WORKSHOP 4

by and for teachers

THE TEACHER AS RESEARCHER
edited by
Thomas Newkirk

HEINEMANN
Portsmouth, New Hampshire

L B1576
WL 7
1992 x

Published by
Heinemann Educational Books, Inc.
361 Hanover Street   Portsmouth, NH 03801-3959
Offices and agents throughout the world

Every effort has been made to contact the copyright holders for
permission to reprint borrowed material where necessary. We
regret any oversights that may have occurred and would be
happy to rectify them in future printings of this work.

ISBN 0–435–108728–2
ISSN 1043-1705

Designed by Wladislaw Finne.

Printed in the United States of America
10   9   8   7   6   5   4   3   2   1

CONTENTS

ABOUT
WORKSHOP 4

I t is fitting that this issue, devoted to the teacher as researcher, should follow the *Workshop* issue devoted to politics, since both issues deal with politics. *Workshop 4* primarily deals with knowledge—and who can claim to make that knowledge. As Glenda Bissex has written, teacher research addresses a central issue of authority: "Who is empowered to see—to research, to know, and be known as an authority" (1987, p. 17).

Teacher research implicitly (and sometimes explicitly) challenges the top-down models that still dominate many areas of education, such as special education and reading. According to these models, Knowledge is created by those removed from the classroom, a cadre of researchers whose job it is to create a set of validated practices or "research base." For example, reading researchers have for years tried to define the proper place of phonics instruction. The classroom teacher works as a technician, "applying" the research in the classroom. In its most extreme forms, the teacher is given a script to follow so that classroom decision making does not interfere with "optimum" performance. The power relationship is clear. Those who do research create knowledge. Teachers merely receive and apply that knowledge.

The situation is similar to the position of midwives in the early nineteenth century. Laurel Ulrich, in *A Midwife's Tale* (1990), describes the tenuous relationship between midwives and the medical profession during this period. At the end of the eighteenth century, midwives in New England had primary responsibility for assisting childbirth and for the treatment of a number of illnesses. Their methods were noninvasive—gargles, poultices, bandages, herbal medicines, compresses, and a great deal of observation. In almost all cases the patient was surrounded by women from the household and area who would talk with and comfort the patient and look for significant changes. Ulrich terms this approach "social medicine"; the treatment was not learned by formal professional training, but by "a slow building up of seemingly casual experience." And to judge from the records of experienced midwives, like Martha Ballard of Hallowell, Maine, social medicine could be highly successful.

But as a result of the emerging professionalism of the male medical establishment, midwives were soon placed under the direction of doctors, and were required to assist in such questionable practices as bloodletting during childbirth and the extensive use of opium. The medical establishment did what any professional organization must do—it denied the value of the local, contextual, and empathetic knowledge that was gained through experience in order to justify a hierarchical structure that it would control.

The parallel with teaching, is, I hope, obvious. To justify a professional research class, it is necessary to show the inadequacy of less-credentialed practitioners, such as teachers or midwives, who gain their knowledge through intimate contact and observation. As Stephen North (1987) has argued, it is also necessary to discredit "lore," the oral and narrative ways that practitioners use to share their knowledge. The teacher-research movement, as I see it, tries to claim this earned knowledge as Knowledge, to see teacher stories as valid ways of making and sharing meaning. To put it yet one more way, the movement aims not to ask teachers to do something they have never done before ("be researchers"), but to validate ways of knowing that have always existed in the culture of schools.

This is not to argue that every teacher story is research; anyone who has spent time in a teachers' room knows that. And not every description of a student is research; description, unless it is part of an inquiry, is simply unfocused data. Finally, not every success story is research, and I believe the rosiness in much of the whole language literature may be keeping us from looking at interesting and unresolved questions. In short, I needed a working definition of teacher research in order to edit this collection. That definition (or at least the key traits) emerged as I read through the submissions.

Teacher research is not a small-scale version of traditional academic research. It is something distinct. Its authority is different. Its approach to citation is different. Its audience is different. While it is crucial for teachers to read widely, the authority of the teacher-researcher comes primarily from experience in the classroom, from questioning, observation, and reflection. Whereas the academic researcher describes questions arising out of prior research, the teacher-researcher describes questions arising out of prior experience. For example, in this collection Boni Gravelle writes about her difficulty of getting all of her students to write stories. Tim Hillmer speaks of his difficulty with the "little professors," the students in his class who don't like fiction. In my view, readers respond not to the published research that Gravelle and Hillmer cite on these problems (and they cite very little), but to the relevance of the problems that each of them address. Readers match their own experiences with that described by the teacher-rescarcher: Have I seen that too? How did I deal with it? Extensive citations of published work often interfere with this process of identification because they undercut the true authority of the researcher.

The relationship of the teacher-researcher to his or her material also differs. Traditionally, the academic researcher maintains a detachment and does not foreground attitudes or emotions in the writing (though this is beginning to change). It is this emotional neutrality, I believe, that alienates teachers from research. The classroom is a place of strong and shifting emotional demands on the teacher, more so now than perhaps at any other time in this country's history. Teacher talk is anything but neutral; it is filled with hope, frustration, delight, anger, and humor. The emotional life of teaching cannot—and should not—be excised from teacher research; in fact, questions often arise out of a sense of something not going right in the classroom. So as I read the submissions, I listened for this engaged voice of the teacher. I believe I heard it in the essays I've chosen, and hope you hear it as well.

There is, however, one quality that unites all researchers, and that is a sense of incompleteness. It's the belief that we will never outgrow our ignorance, that we are blessed with problems we cannot solve. To me, this sense of ignorance is *the* primary motivation for personal development, and is far more potent than "inspirational" talks or writing, most of which leave me feeling curmudgeonly and skeptical. When we ask new questions about our classrooms (and ourselves), we admit the possibility of real self-transformation. To ask if things might be done differently is to loosen the hold of routine and habit.

In reading the manuscripts I looked for those writers driven by this curiosity, and again I believe I found them. But the submissions also revealed a double purpose (and to some degree a cross-purpose). Teacher research typically tries both to argue for an approach (writing conferences, portfolios, group shares) and to explore what students do when they are taught through this approach. The researcher attempts to both persuade and investigate, and in persuading, the temptation to highlight exemplary work is almost irresistible. The failures, the false starts, and the mundane work are hidden from view. The focus is on the more proficient students, while those who encounter difficulty fade into the background.

Clearly, we need to see exemplary work. But if teacher research is a form of inquiry, it needs to use student work as more than evidence of success. We need to include a variety of examples in order to ask questions: What processes led the student to perform in this way? What problems derailed some students but not others? What kind of support might these students need? I feel that by acknowledging these situations, teacher research can be even more persuasive because it will be more realistic and identifiable.

A final criterion for teacher research, as for all research, is that it be made public. Private ruminations, even the talk in the teachers' room (no matter how stimulating), does not place the teacher in that more public space the researcher needs to occupy. We have all, of course, been brilliant in private. But when we have had to speak as an authority beyond an accepting audience—particularly that most accepting of audiences, ourselves—we see ourselves in a new light. We enter a broader community. We put our ideas and practices on public display. We read our words and marvel at the self-confidence, the sheer bluff, of the writer. The contributors to this volume, most of whom see their words in print for the first time, will be changed by that public experience. It has been my honor, as editor, to work with them on these very public words.

T.N.

References

Bissex, Glenda. 1987. "Why Case Studies." In *Seeing for Ourselves: Case Study Research by Teachers of Writing*, ed. Glenda Bissex and Richard Bullock. Portsmouth, NH: Heinemann.

North, Stephen. 1987. *The Making of Knowledge in Composition: Portrait of an Emerging Field*. Portsmouth, NH: Heinemann.

Ulrich, Laurel. 1990. *A Midwife's Tale: The Life of Martha Ballard, Based on Her Diary*. New York: Vintage.

TEACHER-RESEARCHER-STORYTELLER

TIM GILLESPIE
Multnomah County
Education Service District
Portland, Oregon

*B*rimming with pride, the first grader rushed across the classroom to share what he had just written. He held the piece of paper out to his teacher and asked her to read it. She looked at his laboriously-penciled composition:

I Wt to Cadl

"Okay," she began, "I want to. . ."

"Went to," he corrected.

"Went to . . . um, let's see here. Cadl. Cattle? You went to *cattle*, honey? Did you go to a farm or a ranch and see some cattle or something?"

"No, no," said the young author. "It says, 'I went to *Se-attle*'!"

"Oh, *Seattle*," said the teacher. "You went to Seattle."

"No," said the child. "We really went to Issaquah, but I don't know how to spell that."

My friend Colin Dunkeld told me this story, and we laughed together over it. He heard it from a teacher who had heard it from another teacher, and I have since shared it with other teachers. In such a manner, this little story knits us together. Granted, it may be only regional in its humor. In my corner of the country, the Pacific Northwest, we are used to these Native American place-names, and most listeners are aware that the small town of Issaquah, Washington is close to the big city of Seattle. But when all that explanation is necessary, it puts molasses in the story's flow. I have retold the story in other communities, however, and I have discovered it still has the power to connect teachers in the recognition of a small experience we

13

share when teaching children to write, that sort of moment when good sense and English spelling veer away from each other. This recognition—partly bemused, partly resigned—confirms our kinship as teachers and transcends the local nature of the story. Furthermore, the story almost always sets off a cycle of stories in response. Story begets story, a kind of yarnswappers' "Can you top this?" cycle of classroom tales, all on the amusing perils of spelling for young writers.

The main point I want to make, however, is that when I first read research on inventive spelling, it made sense because I had this story and others like it for context. The research was animated by teaching stories; without the stories, the data would have been unrecognizable or, at best, lifeless. Part of our job as teacher-researchers, then, is to collect and remember classroom stories.

Educational scholarship makes certain claims on our attention, but whenever research findings or pedagogical theories are divorced from teachers' stories, those claims will meet resistance or disbelief. If educational theorists or policymakers cannot embody their ideas in true classroom stories, they will suffer the justifiable skepticism of their listeners. As a teacher, I *have* to test research and theory against the professional lore I have accumulated. If I don't, I will be alienated from my experience and my professional community. In this light, the common strain of teacher cynicism about educational research or theory is not so much anti-intellectualism as a deeply-held loyalty to the culture of teachers, and thus a greater trust in teacher stories.

Lurking nearby is an important question: How is it we come to know what we know about teaching? Some teachers I work with chewed this question over recently, and we came up with and classified a long list of sources of our professional knowledge. We identified many forms of *received* knowledge about our craft—formal teacher training we have undergone, in-services and workshops we have attended, and professional books and articles we have read. We identified forms of *earned* knowledge—what we know from our own personal experiences as teachers and as learners. And we identified forms of *shared* knowledge—what we know from our fellow teachers in the form of professional talk and shared observations with our friends across the hall and other respected peers. When I asked these teachers which kinds of knowledge seemed to have had the greatest influence on them, I heard many different answers, but most centered on the knowledge earned and shared in the community of classroom teachers—and a fair amount of this knowledge comes in the form of stories.

My wife, a veteran classroom teacher of almost twenty years, has often told this story: Early in her career, she taught second grade in inner-city Oakland, California. Many of her students lacked experiences outside of the city, so in the winter she decided to organize a Saturday snow trip to the mountains for her class. She rounded up parents, friends, and anyone else she knew with a car who was willing to drive from Oakland up into the California Sierras. The caravan took off early one Saturday morning, and after a couple of hours the group found a worthy hill, thick with snow for sledding, snowball-chucking, and snowman-making. Children were quickly out of the cars and playing in the snow, some for the first time. Later, Jan noticed one of her students, Freddy, gingerly tiptoeing *barefoot* across the snowy field, holding his shoes, socks, and rubber boots. It seems that his boots had filled with snow and the canvas tennis shoes underneath had gotten soaked, so this seven-year-old had taken everything off his frigid feet to dry his shoes and socks out. Now, teeth chattering, Freddy just wanted to get back into one of the warm automobiles and thaw out his toes. "It's cold and wet," he said incredulously, partly in pain and partly in amazement at his discovery. "I didn't know it was cold and wet!"

Freddy's cold feet confirmed Jan's understanding of the vast differences in experience between students, and between teachers and students, and of the powerful part experience plays in what we think of as knowledge. Earlier that fall, some of the children in Jan's class had difficulty with the vocabulary word "village" when it appeared on a standardized reading test. Most of her students, she felt, knew the word from stories they had read or heard, and she was convinced most had a clear understanding of a village as a small community. Yet some of her pupils missed the item on the mandated test. Perhaps, she conjectured, these children conceived of a village in images of their own West Oakland neighborhood, a construct that would allow them to make sense of most stories in which the word appeared. On the standardized reading test, however, the word was to be connected by a line to an illustration of a snowy New England–type village, a scene far from the hot urban sidewalks of Oakland. Jan's barefoot student, innocent about snow, reminded her just how far.

Years later, when I read contemporary research on the impact of background experience and prior knowledge on reading comprehension, I remembered Jan's story of Freddy. The story gives this pedagogical problem the name of a particular child. In twenty years I have not lost the image of Freddy hopping across the field, bare toes ablaze with the sting of pain and amazement when abstract knowledge has to confront cold truth. What the snow presented to Freddy, that's what stories offer us.

Stories are a check as well as a counterbalance to other information that seeks to influence the way we teach. As a form of educational discourse, a story has different protocols than much research or theory. Let me hazard some admittedly broad statements about some of the traditional rhetorical tendencies of these different forms of educational thinking.

Educational theory, for example, usually strives for general principles, while a story strives for singularity. Theory assumes consistency, a story assumes surprise. Theory abstracts, but a story refuses to. Theory is the elegant truth of simplification, a story the messy truth of complication.

Much research, particularly of the traditional empirical sort, searches for generalizations, while a story searches for particularizations. Research hunts for the tellingly large statistic, but a story hunts for the significantly small testimony. Research aims at a meaningfully unified result, but a story allows multiple meanings and interpretations. We read research for answers but stories for problems. Research hopes for a conclusion, while stories often tell us there are no permanent conclusions in the ongoing narrative of a teaching life. There are always more stories to come.

I am not saying that stories are superior to educational theory or traditional research. To learn to be better teachers, we need generalizations as well as specifications, theories to make sense of our stories, a sense of consistency as well as a sense of surprise. One of our responsibilities as teachers, I believe, is to demonstrate how to be good learners. For this reason, we need to pay attention to all the information we can get about our craft, in whatever form it comes. Good learners—wise teachers—are prodigious in their appetite for knowledge from any source. We don't want to neglect any way of knowing, and stories are not the only way to learn.

My colleague Jane Braunger heard a story from a Portland teacher with whom she was working. It seems this fourth-grade teacher wanted her students to have an experience writing a research report on some topic. In explaining the guidelines for the project, she warned the children against copying information directly from the encyclopedia and gave them some advice about avoiding this common kind of plagiarism. The students chose their report topics, and began their research.

After the reports were turned in, the teacher began reading through them one night. One report in the pile particularly troubled her. The student had chosen to write on the solar system. In the report, he mentioned that our solar system has *six* planets. The teacher wondered how on earth the young writer had come up with that bit of misinformation, speculating as to how old the reference materials he used might have been. In class the next day, she asked him about his statement and where he'd gotten his fact.

"Oh," he said. "Well, when you gave us the assignment, you said when we found some information in the encyclopedia we shouldn't just copy it down but that we should change some of the words here and there. You know, change it around a little, put it in our own words. So that's what I did."

Things *can* go awry when we "put it in our own words." Stories have their dangers, as do all forms of knowledge. Stories can be false, and we must guard against the spellbinding allure of well-told stories that misrepresent the truth. In education, for example, we often hear "miracle cure" stories in which some method or product or heroic teacher has wrought instant changes and unqualified successes, and they stir us to unrealistic hope at the same time that they sound vaguely suspicious. We need to recognize the limits of stories, and listen with an ear for their fidelity to our own experience. And when we do our own teacher research, when we collect stories from our own classrooms, we must be careful to see the whole story, to notice and describe the problems and exceptions as well as the triumphs, to be wary of language leading us away from complexity or specificity, which are the hallmarks of good stories. Recognizing the dangers of storytelling, we should nonetheless demand that any claims of educational theory and research, our own included, be amply grounded in classroom stories.

There is one final reason that the knowledge that comes from teacher stories is particularly credible and useful to us, and that has to do with the attitude of the teller.

The language of much educational scholarship, the academic

language of much educational theory and research, is the language of authority. It is language that is trying to prove, assert, and convince. It often sounds like the language of someone who is in power or who wants to be in power. The reader's response is to accept or resist or forge some critical combination of the two.

The language of a story is very different from this language of authority. It is the language of community. Stories are shared. They are collegial. The reader's response is to participate. Stories invite that participation by beckoning the next story, the echo story. Much pedagogical language is in the form of a claim; stories take the form of an invitation. As such, stories are profoundly democratic. The pause at the end of a story is an old and elemental silence: Whose voice will be heard next?

Small wonder, then, that teachers have so readily embraced the work of educational ethnographers and descriptive researchers, or that teachers have jumped to add their own stories to the collection of teacher-researcher accounts. The scholarship of Donald Graves is enthusiastically accepted because it is rich with classroom stories of children that sound real, children we recognize. Nancie Atwell's advice sounds more like the kind of practitioner knowledge we regularly share with one another than the pronouncement of a remote expert. Their stories honor the narrative wisdom of teachers. Simultaneously, we remain skeptical of programs, systems, research, and theories that do not include stories that make sense to us, skeptical of those who speak to us from the heights of authority rather than from the ranks of community.

I read a story by Lynn K. Rhodes some years ago in the National Council of Teachers of English journal *Language Arts*. I will retell it as I remember it, before looking it up, mindful that I may have some small details wrong in my memory or that I may have expanded the story a bit beyond its original size and shape.

A second grader named Rita was having a great deal of trouble with writing, and she was sent to a special program to get some extra help. The teacher in charge, needing to do an initial diagnosis, talked to Rita briefly and discovered that writing didn't make much sense to Rita and that she didn't like it much. Then the teacher gave Rita a piece of paper and a pencil and invited her to go off in the corner and write something—anything. A full half hour later, Rita came back and presented her perfect composition: I HAD A CAT.

After Rita had shared the work, the teacher asked why she thought it had taken so long to write this piece. Rita said, "I had to think of a story I knew how to spell."

The teacher nodded, figuring this comment might offer an insight into Rita's struggles. Perhaps Rita believed a writer has to know how to write something perfectly *before* she undertakes it, or that writing is a matter of mastering form rather than crafting meaning.

I imagine then the teacher's next strategy. She begins to ask Rita some questions with the hope of drawing out more information and focusing more on meaning. Perhaps a conversation about the cat will connect Rita more with her story and give her a sense that she has more to say.

"So what kind of cat did you have?" the teacher asks. "What was its name? What color was it? It sounds like maybe you don't have your cat anymore. What happened to it? Could you write more about it?"

Rita looks at the teacher, squirms a bit, and says, "I never had a cat." (Rhodes 1981)

This story is mostly about children and learning to write, but like most good stories, it also welcomes in much more. Rita's story offers me a way to think about teaching writing that includes the image of a hesitant human face and the sound of a small voice. This is the story's greatest value. But it also offers me, by metaphor, a way to think about the value of stories in learning to be a teacher.

Rita's knowledge of writing was divorced from her own meaningful stories. For her, writing was not a matter of sharing and reflecting on her own experience with other members of her classroom community, but rather was a struggle to understand abstract ideas and master a received set of skills. Thus, it was an act that made little sense to her.

In like fashion, our knowledge about teaching must be as much a matter of sharing and reflecting on our classroom experiences with other teachers in our community as it is an act of understanding abstract ideas or mastering pedagogical skills. Our knowledge—our teacher research—must be lavishly illustrated with and habitually embodied in stories. For if our knowledge of teaching, like Rita's knowledge of writing, is divorced from our own meaningful stories, our knowledge will ultimately make little sense.

References

Rhodes, Lynn K. 1981. " 'I Had a Cat': A Language Story." *Language Arts* 58: 773–74.

SILENCES IN OUR TEACHING STORIES: WHAT DO WE LEAVE OUT AND WHY?

THOMAS NEWKIRK
University of New Hampshire
Durham, New Hampshire

I speak on the phone with my parents, who are both in their late seventies. They tell me about the weather, the flowers, my dad's bird project, the Cleveland Browns—but almost never about a topic I most want to know about, their health.

"How are you feeling, Mom?"
"Fine, fine. I feel all right."

My dad gets angry if I even ask about his health, but, fortunately, each loves to talk about the health of the other. Mom will go on about Dad's bronchitis. My father will describe Mom's knee problem. So the trick is to catch one of them alone in the house. It's a quirk in the Newkirk house, one of many. Do not admit to illness. A silence in the narrative.

I'm interested in the silences in our narratives as teachers, the things we are reluctant to discuss. All groups, it seems to me, construct their own conventions for telling stories, just as my family has done. These conventions define what is said and what is unsaid. They determine the appropriate kinds of responses to certain situations—and they indicate reactions or feelings that are inappropriate. They define the "normal."

Problems occur, though, when we don't feel these "normal feelings," particularly when what we feel is less than noble— anger, envy, frustration, inadequacy, disappointment, or lack of affection. Often in cases like these we remain silent, and conclude that there is something wrong with us. To admit these feelings, to tell a different narrative, is to risk being thought weird, perverted, not a good teacher, not a good parent, not a good person.

While I plan to focus on the stories we tell about reading and writing classrooms, I want to begin with a story of motherhood which demonstrates the way we are silenced by conventional cultural myths. The story is called "Myth America" and was written by Karen Weinhold, a participant in the New Hampshire Writing Program.

> For days after the birth of my first child I silently believed that I was an emotional cripple. I felt awe for this new life, tinged with resentment for the intrusion she was making on what little exhausted privacy I had left. But I didn't love her.
>
> When feeding times rolled around I momentarily welcomed the relief from the tedium of the hospital day. Within 10 or 15 minutes I prayed for the nurse to return and take the baby away—I had had enough.
>
> Once at home, I was burdened with the overwhelming responsibility of caring for this squalling bit of humanity. A whole new environment filled with baths, bottles, formulas, diapers, and cradle cap and navel infections insulated me.
>
> Nagging constantly subsurface was my lack of emotional attachment to this child, and I began to seriously consider that I was emotionally unbalanced. Of course, I did not share these feelings with anyone; that would have been totally un-American!
>
> I believed the TV commercials that depicted mother and child rocking in worlds of billowing sheer curtains, sun streaming through quiet dawnings, confidently using the Baby X nurser to achieve this serenity. However, the reality I was living was a grotesque parody of this tranquil scene. The baby woke in the pitch black of night and my body resisted waking, sagging and devoid of maternal joy.

The situation was made worse by unsolicited advice of older women telling Karen that the time of caring for an infant was the best time of a woman's life. For almost three months, Karen carried on this subterfuge, pretending to feel delight.

> Then one day, when she was 11 weeks old, it happened. Quite suddenly, out of nowhere, while I sat on the living room floor watching her in her infant's seat, a smile spread her lips as we made eye contact, and my heart vaulted. It was that simple. There it was . . . what I had been searching for since her birth jumped out and grabbed me. . . . I was amazed.
>
> I spent several days puzzling over this phenomena until the truth hit me over the head. It was not possible for me to love or hate something until I knew it. Even predisposition couldn't create these feelings. Until I had tended to her needs, watching her responses increasing daily under my care, and until I had slowly recognized the emerging personality, detachment prevailed. . . .

I wanted to sing and dance and shout the news to the world. I was not emotionally deranged, merely a late bloomer. The myth of instantaneous maternal love, perpetuated by the media, had been dispelled.

In fact, Karen did not immediately shout her discovery to the world. It was years after the birth of the child that she managed to tell outsiders about the experience. Her story was difficult to tell because it was not the conventional mother-love story.

This is just one of many possible examples of the ways women, historically, are asked to emulate perfection: moral perfection—the perfect nurturer willing to expend any amount of energy for friends and family; physical perfection—matching the images of women in the media, always thin, young, and on the edge of sexual adventure; or, more recently, the image of super-woman—seamlessly combining the roles of household manager, caring mother, loving and passionate wife, and dedicated professional.

These ideals, to the extent that they are unrealistic, inflict psychological damage; they induce guilt, envy, and a sense of inadequacy. A friend of mine compared the situation to Margaret Atwood's book, *The Handmaid's Tale* (1986), where there are two classes of women and it was not always clear who belonged to which class. When my friend sees a woman who seems to be managing career and family, she looks for what she calls a "crack," some kind of lapse. Twinkies *and* Doritos in the packed lunch. A rainy Sunday with the kids fighting when the woman screams she can't take it any more, or breaking a glass in the sink in anger. Once this crack appears, my friend knows they can be friends.

As I read the literature on whole language/writing process classrooms, I wonder if we are not creating the role of "super teacher," one more ideal, without cracks, that creates a sense of inadequacy in all of us. Are there silences in the narratives we tell of our whole language/writing process classrooms? Are we telling everything? Do these consistently upbeat success stories capture the emotional underlife of teaching? I think not.

I confess that I have become increasingly estranged from much of what I now read. There is an emotional turbulence and a frequency of failure in my own teaching that I do not see reflected in many accounts, including ones I have written or edited myself. In the classes I read about, everything seems to work; student writing is impressive, often deeply moving; the teacher seems to have achieved full participation of all members of the class. And, what I find most difficult to believe, the teacher never shows signs of despondency, frustration, anger, impatience, or disappointment. If there is anger or frustration, it is directed at external forces—administrators, testing services, the government (the designated "bad guys")—but never at themselves or their students. The teachers I read about don't doubt their competence, or at least they don't admit to their doubts.

I have all these feelings—mixed with exaltation, pride, affection, and admiration, to be sure. But the dark side is there. There are days when I feel the energy sucked out of me, days in late November when I'm teaching a 4:00 freshman English class. It's that time the Scots call the "gloaming," no longer daylight, but not yet night. Still too early to light a fire. Usually a student turns on the lights, but on some days, the first six or seven students just come in and sit in the growing darkness, exhausted; they don't talk. I come into the room and feel as if there is a great weight I must move, and I'm not always sure I can do it. Sometimes I can't. I think of optimistic claims that all students want to write, need to write—and I think, maybe, but not today.

These days of gloaming are hard enough to deal with, but they are much harder if I feel that no one else experiences what I experience, if I imagine their classes getting off to a sparkling beginning, or if I imagine that they never have the sinking feeling that I am experiencing. If I must imagine myself alone with this problem, my very competence as a teacher is called into doubt.

By now you may sense my own paranoia and insecurity—which is fine. As a non-Catholic I have always been fascinated by the act of confession. As a Presbyterian, I was told to do my talking directly to God, but the distance seemed too great. The closest thing I experience to confession, now, is my semiannual trip to the dentist where I'm asked if I floss regularly and I must admit, eyes averted, that I don't. I plan to continue here in this confessional vein, hopeful that there will be some glimmers of recognition in what I say, but recognizing that by the end you may find me a true neurotic.

I'd like to tell a failure story. It is a story about a student that I will call Lisa who took my freshman English class. A goalie on the women's hockey team, and outspoken and responsive in class, Lisa demonstrated real skill in her early assignments in the class—even though she hadn't had much success in high school as a writer.

For one of the early in-class writings, I read a passage from Russell Baker's autobiography, *Growing Up* (1982), describing a teacher, Mr. Fleagle, who generally failed to hold the classes' attention, but who helped Baker discover his ability to write essays. I asked Lisa, and others in the class, to think about a teacher who had affected them. Lisa picked an English teacher, Mrs. Jill Howard, who had earned the nickname "Jill-basa" at a pep rally. Here is how Lisa described it:

> Before the time I did at Conant Regional High School, cheerleaders hesitated to set foot inside our gym. Having no cheerleaders of our own, the occupants of our high school took great delight in making basketball games a living hell for any daring squad accompanying an opposing team. Despite the fact that we didn't have any cheerleaders, our principal insisted that pep rallies were a necessity to inspire a basketball team to the coveted title of state champions.
>
> During one of these infamous pep rallies, some of the men in the teaching staff thought it would be funny, if not inspiring, to dress as cheerleaders and cheer for the team. Mrs. Howard would probably have handled the idea of three grown men parading in front of a huge mob of screaming kids, wearing mini-skirts and wigs. But when these men blew up balloons and stuck them up their already tight sweaters, Mrs. Howard was driven into another one of her women's rights campaigns. She was outraged. The straw that broke the camel's back was when one of the teachers, in an attempt to be cute, turned the balloons so that the stems pointed out, achieving the "bra-less" look.
>
> She flew out of the bleachers and pointed out to the superintendent how immature and disrespectful her male cohorts were being. The superintendent tried to accuse her of taking things too personally and told her she should loosen up a little. Then she began yelling, "If you think a woman's mammary glands are so funny, would you be amused if I paraded in front of the student body with a Kielbasa down my pants?"
>
> In her fury Mrs. Howard failed to notice that she was screaming in the direction of the microphone. The entire gym was silent as Mrs. Howard made her point. The men in the cheerleader outfits were not willing to be humiliated that easily, thus Jill Howard was dubbed "Jillbasa."
>
> . . . I had great admiration for the way she stood up against the entire school. When I hear her good-naturedly being called "Jill-basa" by a fellow staff member, or behind her back by some wise ass student, I have nothing but respect for her.

I admired the same thing in Lisa's writing that she admired in Mrs. Howard. I liked her boldness, her clear feminist point of view (not common among New Hampshire eighteen-year-olds). I liked the way she could snap off this anecdote. Based on this paper, and her next one on what it was like to play goalie for the *boys'* hockey team at her high school, I sensed (and I think she sensed) her skill as a writer. It seemed like it might be one of those rare times when a student finds a major, even a vocation.

But things fell apart. In the last part of the course, students were to write one paper involving research and another responding to a novel. Lisa, as I recall, set out to write a fictional account in which she worked in information about steroid use at the University of New Hampshire. I remember my sinking feeling as I read her first draft. The incidents seemed contrived, uninteresting, and she seemed to be presenting no information. I remember suggesting that she interview some of the athletes on the university's sports teams and that she consider not using this fictional approach—because it didn't seem to be working for her. In my enthusiasm, I'm sure my suggestion sounded like a direction. My nudge was more of a shove.

The paper never developed; a few bits of information were inserted into her account. And I could feel that the collaborative spirit of our conferences on the early papers was gone. Her work on the last paper was perfunctory. On her evaluation for the course, she complained about me telling her how her papers should be written, rather than allowing her to write the paper she wished to write. It was painful to read at the time, painful to recount now.

As I thought of my work with Lisa, I realized, now four years later, that I had missed an important clue to working with her. In her paper on becoming a goalie on the male team, she talked about the men—her father and the principal—who had discouraged her from trying to make the team. She wrote about how she had had to ignore their advice, and how she had proven she could handle the job. It is now clear that she saw me as one more man who was trying to divert her from what she wanted to do. She had told me that the great lesson of her life was not to be diverted, and I had missed the warning.

A quick, and I believe faulty, lesson to derive from this failure story is the need to grant the student "ownership," a term that belies the complex relationships we have with students. According to the ownership interpretation, I took over the paper, and the student became alienated from her own writing. In other words, I had neglected one of the basic tenets of the writing process movement. But, in practice, working with students is never so simple as applying basic rules. There are times when I have had to be directive in exactly the same way I was with Lisa. I recall a student who had decided to write a research paper on "Russia" but came back because the library didn't have anything on his topic. That student didn't need me to hang back; he needed some fairly explicit guidance.

In Lisa's case, the issue was much more complex than applying the rule "give students ownership." I had to balance objectives that conflicted in some way. On one hand I wanted her to make choices in her writing and to feel the sense of control that comes with making choices. *I also wanted her to succeed.* The situation became difficult when her choices seemed to be taking her in a direction that, at least to me, would not result in a satisfactory paper. It was a close call—and I blew it.

It was a close call in the way that many of our tough decisions are close calls. Our thirteen-year-old daughter wants to take the bus to an evening movie at the mall. How do we as parents balance our (and her) desire for her to be independent with a concern for her safety? We say no. But it was close. If many of our decisions as teachers are close calls, it is inevitable that we will often make the wrong choice. But who writes about these close calls, these decisions we would like to have back? If all I hear is complacent silence, do I conclude I am the only one with regrets?

I'd like to suggest some ways we can tell new stories which explore the issues that the success stories leave out.

1. Create forums for telling failure stories. We all have them. Let's talk about them. At the staff meetings at the University of New Hampshire we found that we were trapped in success stories—everything worked. So one day we scheduled a meeting which we entitled "Bombs." Everybody had to come with a failure story, and we began with the most experienced staff, including the director.
2. There is another kind of story, related to the failure story, that may be even more important for our psychic balance—those we tell to celebrate absurdity. Tim Gillespie's essay in this section includes several. These stories are not necessarily about failure, but about the ways in which our teaching doesn't always work out the way we planned. Here's one from the early writing process research that Don Graves conducted.

A first grader, I'll call her Emily, had just finished her story on her birthday party. It went something like this: "I had a party. It was fun. We did lots of things." The teacher schooled in appropriate response said, "It sounds like your party was fun"—and then began to probe. What kinds of things did you do? Did you have a cake? What kind? What was your favorite present? After Emily supplied a few answers, the teacher said, "Don't you think a reader would want to know these things?"

Emily replied, "I've got an idea. If some people in the class want to know more about my parties, I'll invite them to the next one." She closed her book and didn't add a word.

Stories like these keep us sane and humble. We laugh—but at the same time are reminded that things don't always work as we planned. They celebrate the unpredictability of teaching. For me, they are that "crack" I spoke of earlier, the opening that allows for companionship.

3. Teachers should regularly visit the classes of other teachers. When I was teaching high school I was appalled at how little cross-classroom visiting went on. I imagined that elementary schools, because they were smaller, did a better job at this. I'm now convinced I was wrong. In most schools there seems to be almost no visiting. Districts seem far more willing to let teachers come to conventions where we can talk in airless rooms at some remove about teaching.

Visiting helps us all learn new ways of teaching, but, I feel, it also can give us more realistic models of success than we get from the success stories that we read. I remember when the first work on the writing process was coming out, with all the kids loving to write all the time. I had trouble picturing the classroom. It didn't sound like any classrooms I'd been in. When I visited one of the project classrooms, there were a couple of boys playing in the sandbox during writing time. I'm not suggesting it wasn't a fine and innovative class. It was. But I was so grateful, so relieved to see those boys—who could care less about writing—in the sandbox.

4. Finally, those who write and make presentations about writing can try to be more balanced in the examples of student work we present. I know from experience that the temptation to highlight extraordinary work is almost irresistable, particularly if we are trying to convince people that our approach works. But I feel we can do a better job by showing some less than exemplary examples, too.

I would like to mention one book that has told these new stories better than any other book I know—Sondra Perl and Nancy Wilson's *Through Teachers' Eyes* (1986). The book is a collection of portraits of teachers who had worked in a writing project. The authors made the bold move of describing a successful teacher, Ross Burkhardt, who had a bad year. He never established a good working-relationship with the students. The more things did not seem to work the more he pressed; the more he pressed the worse the relationship became. At the end of the year a student wrote, "I think you shouldn't get as close [to the class] as you were this year because in every class you have there is always someone trying to give you hell." Sondra Perl wrote:

> Giving Ross hell. The words stuck. . . . The students had given him a year of hell. They tried his patience, exhausted his will, defeated his spirit. And by the end of the year they had won. On the last day of school, unlike so many years past, Ross organized no final culminating class, wrote no poem to commemorate the occasion, staged no play to perform in—perhaps the most telling sign of defeat. (p. 144)

In writing Ross's portrait, Perl was faced with a dilemma. Ross learned from his bad year, his style of leadership changed, and he regained the commitment of his students. But Perl had this data from his bad year. She wrote about her problem:

> Yet in those years, as Ross regained his footing, I continued to write about the year he lost it. Occasionally, when I showed him drafts, I wondered whether he wouldn't have wished that I rewrite history, soften a description, rework a particular incident. Yet throughout all our meetings, Ross was remarkably consistent, saying—and meaning—that if there were something in his struggle that might be of value to other teachers, then I should tell his story as I was doing, no holds barred. Several years later, I am still struck by his willingness to allow me to use his story to serve others. (p. 148)

If we are looking for heroes, I nominate Ross Burkhardt. And I hope that he will be remembered not as the teacher who suffered through a bad year, but as the teacher who wanted the story of that year told—"no holds barred." May we all be as honest in telling the stories of our teaching.

As I was preparing this essay I showed a draft of it to Karen Weinhold, the author of the piece on mother-love that I quoted earlier. A couple of weeks later she sent me a draft of an essay about her teaching of writing. Karen had become major innovator in her district, but the piece focused on peer response groups—they'd never worked well for her. What struck me was the confessional tone of the piece. It was as if she was admitting a sin that she'd kept hidden for years. Groups had never worked for her. Conferences, yes. But not groups. She'd shared her secret with some of her colleagues, and each of them had a secret, too. One was uncomfortable with teaching absolutely no grammar. Another found her record-keeping system took so much time that she never read on her own. Silences. Secrets.

It's time they stopped being secrets. It's time we tell the whole story of our teaching. No holds barred.

References

Atwood, Margaret. 1986. *The Handmaid's Tale.* Boston: Houghton Mifflin.

Baker, Russell. 1982. *Growing Up.* New York: Condon and Weed.

Perl, Sondra and Nancy Wilson. 1986. *Through Teachers' Eyes: Portraits of Writing Teachers at Work.* Portsmouth, NH: Heinemann.

Weinhold, Karen. "Myth America." Unpublished manuscript written for the 1981 New Hampshire Writing Program.

THE ETHICS OF OUR WORK IN TEACHER RESEARCH

PATRICIA JOHNSTON
Centennial School District
Warminster, Pennsylvania

*I*n *Living by the Word*, Alice Walker (1988) recalls a parent's outrage in the early eighties over the use of her novel, *The Color Purple*, in a high school literature class. The parent objected to Celie's language, stating that this " 'exposure' of their folk language" (Walker 1988, p. 55) was degrading to blacks. Walker's counter and her own view of language is impressive: "If we kill off the *sound* of our ancestors, the major portion of us, all that is past, that is history, that is human being is lost, and we become historically and spiritually thin, a mere shadow of who we were, on the earth" (1988, p. 62). Her words resonate with concerns I have had over the body of literature that makes up the field of teacher-research. I am concerned with what gets said in stories of classroom practice, yes, but I am more concerned with what does not get said. As many have said so elegantly before me (and only through them and because of them do I have my say), teacher-research is a human and humane activity. I merely suggest a few observations made from my own experience as a teacher-researcher that speak to the humanity of our work.

When I began my own study of eighth graders in the winter and spring of 1987, I was unprepared for many things. Some of the surprises concerned the doing of teacher-research. Much of what I did not expect, however, resulted from what I did as a teacher-researcher when the official research was over. I had a summer to think about what my students and I had done together, to analyze data, to write, and to gather my thoughts. I took time to stop and be still. It is in that period of quiet that I learned to be consciously reflective about my practice, my attitudes, my theories, and my beliefs. I began to articulate what I felt had been intuitively or instinctively correct. I also began to see what is problematic about my own work in teacher-research. Without telling the whole story—the discovery as well as the underside—our narratives will be thin, weakened, a distillation of teachers' voices when we in classrooms, in fact, know the whole picture.

This look at the ethics of our work is grounded in certain assumptions of teacher-research. First, the activity of teacher-research frames the reality of the classroom. Questions for inquiry focus attention on particular activities within the scene of day-to-day practice. Like fences that let us know what's in or out, teacher-research designates borders for investigation or study. Second, research is an intervention. I learned that as we elect to go into a classroom with a stance different from our traditional role as a teacher, we are interrupting the reality of ourselves and others. Third, teacher-research is a particular kind of intervention. We need to explore the nature of that intervention, examine our methods, and take responsibility for the consequences of our interruption.

A First Consideration: Vulnerability in Participation

The six thirteen-year-olds of my study volunteered to take part in Best Books, the literature program that I taught. As part of the routine of the program, students left their English classrooms once every eight school days to meet with me to discuss books that all had agreed to read. We were, from the onset, a small group. In time, we became a close group. Part of this closeness is due to the function of the program that I taught. Students were reading books of young-adult literature chosen because they were discussable. That is, the texts all had to do with adolescents in problematic situations where decisions had to be made. The murkiness of the decision-making process invited student response.

My contention, however, is that the way the group developed was determined, in part, because of the research intervention. At our first meeting I had to inform students of my research project. They were given guidelines about what their participation would include: formal and informal personal interviews, reading protocols, tape recordings of book discussions, journal writing, and family interviews. This seemed rather like a business arrangement to me until I came to realize that my students, appropriately enough, had to deal with their roles as research subjects. The friend of one of my students stopped me cold by saying: "Oh, I know what you're doing. You're conducting reading protocols. Melissa Ann [my student in the program] told me all about that."

I wonder now how I could have expected anonymity within the school, how I did not understand that these six students were perceived by their peers as special or apart from their classmates. They struggled with questions of their own unique place in the school because of their involvement in this work. Asheley (another student in the group) commented that classmates wanted to know what we were doing when we met together; the friends of my students were curious about my tape recorder. Another of my students, Robert Smith, asked if people would read about them, and if I spoke about the study with my own classmates and professors. The amount of time my students gave to the project and my evening visits with their families in their homes caused me to wonder if I had, in fact, asked more of my students than they were ready to give. How did they deal with the curiosity of friends about comprising a selected group? How were they perceived by others in their class, and what effect did this have on the development of the six readers as an interpretive group? I am profoundly concerned with the probability that the work of this study had effects on others that I had not anticipated. Did I help to foster a kind of insider/outsider split in a class; if so, in what ways did this exacerbate adolescent insecurities?

Though I had set out to engage in the naturalistic observation of a classroom scene, I had inadvertently cropped the picture I was taking (see Johnston 1989). Though I wanted and intended not to upset standard procedures of schooling, the introduction of my perspective as teacher-researcher actually set boundaries. I had a particular gaze that was focused by my research questions. Those boundaries, in turn, affected the development of my group.

In addition, I was taken by surprise by the vulnerability that I felt as a researcher. The role of participant-observer is not the distanced and dispassionate persona that I had imagined. I now walked into my school each day as a researcher as well as a teacher, and that made differences I had not anticipated. Though I continued to carry still-ungraded homework papers through the school door each weekday morning, I brought with me, too, the paraphernalia of a researcher: extra cassette tapes, journals for field notes, and protocol texts. With a heightened awareness, I now sat in assemblies, read daily announcements, watched interactions among students, and listened to conversations on my planning time. My new awareness stemmed from my need to give shape to what I saw and heard and felt, to an ongoing sense of being in the unfamiliar. Though I continued to work in the building where I had first started teaching sixteen years before, I navigated the unknown daily as I questioned standard practices and procedures. In my attempt to look closely at systems within the school, I prodded others to reconsider their definitions of schooling and, therefore, implicated students, families, and teachers in my search. I felt total responsibility for what I had begun and for what our work together could uncover.

Further, there were shifts in relationships within the school community as a result of my research intervention, which contributed to my feelings of being alone in an academic pursuit and out on a limb. In interviews with colleagues, for instance, I was the interviewer, the person with the questions. Although I saw my work as collaborative at the time, my distanced analysis tells me that I held the research agenda. The notes and tapes, the record of the conversations, went with me as I left the room. Working with friendly colleagues did not absolve my awareness of difference and my feelings of isolation. I felt vulnerable because in many ways I was the "other." In one instance, a professional with departmental responsibilities involving the students of my study sought to put an end to the research. My research involved entrance to a particular English classroom and that, she argued, was her domain. Through a higher intervention the study continued, but I was left shaken for a time. I was perceived as the "intruder," and I truly was vulnerable.

More disturbing, however, was a realization that my deeply invested notions about what happens in classrooms were being blown apart: I alternately was and was not the listener I envisioned myself to be; I was less tolerant to forms of resistance than I had credited myself with; and not all educators are either colleagues or advocates for children.

I had a running commentary of the events, attitudes, and remarks of my day. All was monitored. All was processed. The very act of doing the research, reflecting on my own practice, attending to what might otherwise be ignored in light of hall passes and announcements and misplaced memos, was different than I had imagined. The field notes became a place of discovery and learning and professional growth. Like any good learning, the reality of the doing is that, at times, it left me overwhelmed. I was often perplexed by a growing understanding of my personal inability to affect change and of the enormity of problems and circumstances over which I had no control: I did not set the staff development agenda; I was not a participant in curriculum decision making; I had no voice in determining policy; and I had no vehicle for influencing the messages about learning and literacy that students bring to school from home. At times I regained perspective and felt energized by the possibilities of contribution and conversation. At other times the physical toll of continually being alert, aware, and analytical by categorizing and classifying the events of the day left me numb.

As a graduate student I had a network of a university-sanctioned committee and colleagues who were immersed in issues similar to my own to help me deal with my vulnerability. I had a place to go where I could commiserate; I had a language that helped me express what I felt in terms of what I observed, and I was not alone. Obviously, all of these feelings and actions had important effects on me and my students—we were all vulnerable. The reality of sitting in a room with an eighth grader as she or he thinks aloud is about trust and relationships and a sense of "I'm teaching you, teacher. You've given me this chance and I'm going to take you at your word. This is what I think and this is what I feel." The literature in teacher-research has not addressed this kind of response or situation very well. My students were asking me to take them seriously as intellectuals and as coconspirators in a message about learning, a message that might reach other teachers, so that these students could be a part of making changes. We were not prepared for this generosity of spirit, mind, and involvement. I felt responsible as I was committed to the task, yet aware of what I had committed others to as well.

A Second Consideration: Parents

I had always been concerned about home-school relations, but never so much as during those days in 1987 when I sat in the living rooms and kitchens of my students' parents. I learned that most parents are deeply concerned about reading because they care about how their children will manage in a world they see as increasingly less sympathetic to what they value. They want their children to be able to derive pleasure from and to be moved by literature. Parents want their children to care about their thoughts, and to have those ideas shaped and nurtured through books.

The information that parents gave me was, in instance after instance, other than I had expected. The interviews moved to conversation which, in turn, seemed to encourage argumentation. Families appeared to talk freely, offering opinions grounded in examples. They told me what was wrong with the schools, what was good with the schools, what they thought the schools should be doing, and what they expected and feared for their children. And then I left them. I see these parents in September at Back-to-School Night for as long as they have younger children in the junior high school. We meet again at the ninth-grade awards assembly in June and we talk and acknowledge that this may be the last time we have official reason to get together. Why is this leave-taking not a part of our literature? If it causes a wrenching feeling for one researcher, then don't others experience similar feelings? If others do, what does that mean for our research? What do we need to know about intervention in the homes of our students for the sake of research?

My concerns are not about sentimentality. They are about creating an agreement among teacher-researchers that we ask ourselves what we are really doing when we become involved in persons' lives for research purposes. I suggest that I have not served the six families of my research in a manner that befits my understanding of the role of teacher-researcher. Other than writing about my study so that I represent parental views ethically and honestly, I am at a crossroads. Although I have now a research and professional agenda that moves toward the bridging of home and school, the focus is on me and my work, not the people who helped me to get to this place. I am aware that I have asked people to be open with me about their problems without leaving them a solution, a hope of a solution, or even a vehicle to create a solution. I have entered, taken what I needed, and driven away. The balance is in my favor; I was not prepared for this admission or its consequences.

The balance warrants correction, and causes me to wonder what I can offer to the families of my students. I wonder, as well, what I have learned from my experience that can be helpful to other teacher-researchers. I believe that I owe the families something—a next step. At this juncture it seems to me that I assumed that research had limitations in space and time; it seemed a finite term. Now I see that research is generative; it is about "researching," an ongoing task of commitment to a problem, searching for clues to understanding, and a realization about the tentative nature of answers. The result of researching is that I now have more informed questions. I engaged six families in this search; they now deserve to be involved in the working out of these reformulated questions and growing concerns; their voices must be heard in determining the direction of future work. No longer do I see the parents of my six students as names in acknowledgments or footnotes or citations. These parents, as do the students in my study, represent the body of the work; they are the substance of the next step. I found that the relationship is not over just because the interview ended. Instead, there must be a fluidity to our work and a reciprocity to our research if we are to ever come full circle.

A Third Consideration: The Researcher

There is something to be said for teacher-researchers whose own classrooms are their "laboratory," the places where questions about practice are asked, where data is collected, and where findings get played out against theory. First, we are part of a particular school system, full members of the institutions we represent in our research with all the benefits befitting membership. We know the routines, and, to some degree, understand why systems operate the way they do. We are committed to the work of our classrooms and to revising our curricula based on our documented findings, and we are likely to return in September when the data is collected and notes transcribed. Second, we are part of the fabric of the community beyond our specific school. We feel the same pain the community feels when a student is in an accident; we eat breakfast at the local diner; we are "locals"; we follow the high school football team in the fall and the baseball team in the spring; and we run into our students at the mall. What I am saying is that we have knowledge that others who are mere observers could never know. We feel as much a part of our schools as the bricks and mortar.

The current literature on teacher research as well as my own experience tells me that this kind of privileged information is advantageous; it fosters description made from a perspective that outsiders could not have. However, the summer of 1987 was to be a most difficult time of analysis and interpretation for me. What surprised me was that my difficulty was due, in part, to my place in the school, the district, and the community where I conducted my work.

When my friend told me stories in the faculty room that

enrich the history of the community, but also could recall painful memories for others, how do I write the narrative? When my colleague answers an interview question and his comments scare me, how do I represent my colleague in my research? Though I had previously conducted an ethnographic study and was versed in the methods of qualitative analysis, I had to do some soul-searching before I did any writing. The metaphor that guided my systematic review of data was borrowed from Frederick Erickson (1986): analysis is a search for "local meanings," that is, what the occasion meant to the participants in the group. In my search for patterns and categories in the data I discovered that each document, each field note, and each transcription was much like a text to be read. I became aware of the necessary interpretive quality of data analysis. This act of interpretation is, I learned, profoundly biased, and has a specific philosophy that designs the research, that asks the research questions, that selects events as reportable, and that documents presentation.

Hence, teacher-researchers who act as both participants and observers in their own classrooms cannot assume either that they work from positions of neutrality, or that the activity of research is neutral. Research is intervention. Moreover, research is intervention laden with the philosophy and persuasion of the researcher. I realize, for instance, that I will probably always look at classroom activity in terms of its social construction. My earliest questions about teaching had to do with the players in the classroom. I was interested in the relationship between individual and collective meanings with their webs of contextual complexity. This approach influences the way I teach and has probably determined what I teach. It is also what I value.

My analysis is influenced by not only my own predisposition, but by the fact that, though I spend my winter and spring collecting data, I will return to my job as a teacher in September. I will work with my colleagues, the same people who graciously gave their time in formal and informal interviews and whose tapes I transcribed in July. When I report on the community in which I work I acknowledge that I choose my words with care. After all, I shop in the community, have my car serviced there, and have come to depend on the support received over the years from many who live there. When I discuss the school where I teach and the district where I work I am mindful that I am also writing to a school board who makes a check payable to me every two weeks. These are not small issues in teacher-research; they are simply not the focus of discussion in our final research.

A Final Consideration

After returning to the classroom for three years, teaching educators in another setting, and supervising curriculum development in my school district, I see that all forms of my work reflect the curious gaze of the researcher. I have my formal projects, my layered inquiry into practice and theory. I have my informal questions that come at unexpected times and move me to try something different. I also have those serendipitous moments when my students and I discover something together. The winter of 1989 brought such a moment as my seventh graders and I read E. L. Konigsburg's *From the Mixed-Up Files of Mrs. Basil E. Frankweiler* (1967). Claudia and Jamie run away from home because they know they are unappreciated. Their hideout is the Metropolitan Museum of Art. The adventure takes them to Mrs. Frankweiler, who is an eccentric woman of eighty-three years and a patron of the arts. Mrs. Frankweiler has kept vast archives of conversations and events in her life; she is, one can presume, both a researcher of sorts and a bit of a teacher. As the story nears its conclusion Mrs. Frankweiler tells the children, "I'm satisfied with my own research on the subject. I'm not in the mood to learn anything new." Claudia counters, "But Mrs. Frankweiler, you should want to learn one new thing every day. We did even at the museum." I like Mrs. Frankweiler's reply.

> No, I don't agree with that. I think you should learn, of course, and some days you must learn a great deal. But you should also have days when you allow what is already in you to swell up inside of you until it touches everything. And you can feel it inside you. If you never take time out to let that happen, then you just accumulate facts, and they begin to rattle around inside of you. You can make noise with them, but never really feel anything with them. It's hollow (Konigsburg 1967, p. 150).

I think that's what Alice Walker means when she referred to a historic and spiritual health. That's what I would like our teacher-as-researcher literature to be known for—its writers valued the time, the sensitivity, and the commitment warranted for the accumulated facts to swell up and to touch everything. If given the opportunity, we can examine the complexities of our work in teacher research. It seems a given that there are no easy answers. There are, however, questions that we share, questions we cannot ignore if we are to become the teachers we once envisioned we could be.

References

Erickson, Frederick. 1986. "Qualitative Methods in Research on Teaching." In *Handbook of Research on Teaching*. 3rd ed., ed. M.C. Wittrock. New York: Macmillan.

Johnston, Patricia. 1989. "A Scenic View of Reading." *Language Arts* 66: 160–70.

Konigsburg, E. L. 1967. *From the Mixed-Up Files of Mrs. Basil E. Frankweiler*. New York: Dell Publishing Co.

Walker, Alice. 1988. *Living by the Word*. New York: Harcourt Brace Jovanovich.

RESEARCH AS
REFLECTION AND
OBSERVATION

In Regie's Garden
AN INTERVIEW WITH REGIE ROUTMAN

MAUREEN BARBIERI
Laurel School
Shaker Heights, Ohio

*R*egie Routman is making a difference. A veteran class-room teacher, reading specialist, learning disabilities tutor, and Reading Recovery teacher, Regie is an avid observer of children and a voracious reader of professional literature. She has written two books, *Transitions: From Literature to Literacy* (1988) and *Invitations: Changing as Teachers and Learners K–12* (1991), each rich in theory, case-study research, and pragmatic teaching strategies that enable teachers to move toward a whole language approach in their classrooms. After spending mornings teaching with teachers in five elementary schools, she continues to teach children reading and writing every afternoon.

We got together one day in June as the late afternoon sun fell through the greenery of her backyard across the purple clematis and onto coffee cups we balanced on our laps. A butterfly landed first on my notepad and later on her shoulder, but its presence did not distract either of us from the topic at hand: challenges facing today's teachers.

MAUREEN: Nancie Atwell received the David H. Russell Award for research this year in Atlanta. Thanking the committee, she said, "By giving me this award, you're saying to classroom teachers everywhere, 'Your observations do count as real research.' " I was wondering about your feelings on this. Do teachers' observations count? And how can teachers' observations make a difference in American education?

REGIE: Yes, I think teachers' observations do count. The problem is that teachers don't know that they count, and that

43

society, administrators, and parents don't yet value or trust teachers' observations. The issue of testing and evaluation is very much tied up in the issue of trust, and the movement toward portfolio assessment is controversial because it's based quite a lot on trusting teacher judgment, student judgment, and teachers' observations.

MAUREEN: How will the community learn to trust us?

REGIE: I think that will happen more and more as we become more knowledgeable practitioners. To be a really careful, knowledgeable observer of children, you have to know what you're looking for. And so, for me, a lot of that whole notion of teacher-as-researcher implies being current in the field, which takes a lot of commitment and a lot of time.

MAUREEN: How do you do it?

REGIE: It's been mostly through professional reading that I've been able to move to a point where I, first of all, trust what I see because I think—Frank Smith has said this many times—we've been trained to be scripted technicians, so we don't even trust what we see.

I know it took me a long time to trust my own observations, at least ten years. I did a lot of reading, and it was validating. At first, I would only trust my observations if, oh yeah, Goodman saw the same thing or Harste said the same thing. It was like, who am I?

MAUREEN: How does this happen that we see ourselves this way—"just a teacher?"

REGIE: Because we have not been empowered. And that's partly our own doing, that we've been passive. We've got to move away from that passivity and take responsibility for our teaching in order to change, in order to become empowered.

But it was really not until I went to my first IRA meeting that I began to see what it was like out there in the larger world. I was in my tiny little cubbyhole of a room as a resource teacher. Then I saw there was research that supported what I was doing. And I think that's really important.

We have to be able to say, "The research supports this." When we moved to a totally integrated spelling program in the school where I'm teaching right now—we did that three years ago—we made that move based on our observations of children, working as whole language teachers, and realizing that the traditional way of teaching spelling was not working. Kids were memorizing rules; they could get a hundred on a test and still not spell.

But if we had just gone to our principal and said, "This is what we've observed, and we're teachers that you respect," that wouldn't have been enough. We had to present her with the research. If I was not well-read, if I did not keep abreast of that research, I don't think that I would have been able to make the innovations that I've been able to make. So I think it's really a combination of observation plus looking at the research.

MAUREEN: Would you talk a little about how you happened to write your first book, *Transitions?*

REGIE: I felt I had to write it. Maybe that's something about being a writer, although at the time I never would have said that I was a writer. I felt that we teachers needed more specific help and that our contexts here were different than the contexts in New Zealand and Australia, and I felt I understood those contexts because I was in the classroom every day.

MAUREEN: You were reading professional journals, observing and reflecting on your own teaching, keeping a journal. Why were you doing that?

REGIE: Well, maybe for me it was part desperation. I was so bored with the control and with being told what to do. I guess I'm a rebel at heart. I come across as a very cooperative, easygoing kind of person, and I suppose I am, but underneath there's definitely the streak of the rebel. I couldn't stand the structure of what I was being asked to do.

MAUREEN: How can teachers learn to trust themselves? How can we count what we see and what we think as having some value?

REGIE: I think that as a profession we lack confidence. You know, we're not given release time where we can collaborate with each other, and when you're making these observations, you can't do them in a vacuum. And one of the things that helped me realize that my observations were valid was being able to go to an international conference and see what other teachers were doing and thinking and talk with them. So I think there have to be more opportunities for collaboration.

MAUREEN: Is it like that in Australia and New Zealand?

REGIE: When somebody asked me what impressed me most about Australia and New Zealand, I said, "Morning tea," and surprised myself. Morning tea happens at 11:00 each day and teachers are released from their classrooms for fifteen minutes. They get together in an open area, and they drink tea and have cookies, and they talk to each other. I was impressed because I saw so many smiling teachers talking to each other.

The whole notion of collaboration and socialization, which we're trying to foster in whole language with children, has to happen with teachers first.

MAUREEN: Is it happening with the teachers you work with?

REGIE: One thing I feel really terrific about is that we have language arts support groups. We've done this now for four years. The teachers come together once a week, so for me it's five meetings, since I'm in five buildings. We discuss issues in our teaching.

A teacher will say, "This is going on in my classroom." or "Look at what somebody else wrote." And someone else will say, "Well, that's wonderful. Can I see that?" and try it out. So there's that validation. I see that as being really useful.

MAUREEN: What are you talking about these days?

REGIE: We're moving toward portfolio assessment, and that never would have happened if we had not come together weekly and talked about it, read articles, hashed it out. We're going into it in the fall.

Many of us are putting together our own portfolios to have ready for the first week of school to share with the kids. That never would have happened just by one teacher reading about it. It was that collaboration, and it came from the teachers.

MAUREEN: What do you see as the future of evaluation in this country? Do you think the move towards national testing is unavoidable?

REGIE: It's avoidable. We as teachers have to be very active and start lobbying and become proactive. Parents relate to the notion of portfolios because they're real. When you show a parent a portfolio of the child's work, the parent can see what the child is doing. A national test is not going to show them anything.

MAUREEN: What other things are on the agenda at these meetings?

REGIE: One of the things we did was invite the makers of the standardized test that we use to come to our support group. We said, "The reading test that we're using does not reflect the current research on reading. Here's the research, and we want you to tell us when you're going to make the test better." And they came in and spoke to us. We felt like we had taken a stand, and they took us seriously.

MAUREEN: Your parents are very supportive, according to your books.

REGIE: Parents have had a major effect in our district. Marianne

Sopko, who was a parent, got a whole publishing program going. She was so impressed with what it did for her son and felt it should go across the district. That's a very, very strong effort. We have in the building where I'm based close to two thousand titles in a room we call "the Web." It's a book room, and the books are all in multiple copies, all inventoried and on computer. We couldn't do it without the parents.

I say to teachers when they tell me, "My principal's not behind me; I'm having a hard time getting books, making changes": get to your parents. Invite your parents in and have them tell the principal how thrilled they are about what you're doing.

I always use the analogy with parents that "you've done everything right in the home. What we're doing is taking the model that you've used—you've congratulated your children, you've accepted approximations in teaching them to speak. And we're taking your model and trying to bring it into the school." And so they understand, then, the whole notion of approximation and invented spelling. Every time we've done a poor job with parent education, we've run into trouble.

MAUREEN: The new book, *Invitations*, addresses teachers from kindergarten through twelfth grade. What's happening in the middle school and the high school in your district?

REGIE: Well, the K–12 concept was really important to me because I think whole language started in the primary grades and sort of got stuck there in the sense that there was nothing specifically written for intermediate teachers. I'd been talking with teachers across the country and was very surprised when I would be invited in by a high school and find out that what we had at the elementary level had so much to offer the high school—for example, the whole notion of choice. Choice is a really big issue in reading and in writing. Moving away from the lecture format.

MAUREEN: Isn't it also valuing what the individual student knows?

REGIE: Oh, absolutely! And trusting the student, that's the hard thing, trusting the student. And what I found from working with teachers in my district and across the country was that the process is the same from kindergarten through twelfth grade. The kindergarten teacher can learn from the senior-high English teacher, and it's just not that different in terms of what we're trying to accomplish in writing and in reading and in getting kids to take control of their own learning. And

I thought it was very important that this book be K–12. We have to be learning from one another. Teachers are hungry for knowledge and for collaboration.

MAUREEN: What do teachers need most?

REGIE: Teachers need most to trust their own intuition, I think.

MAUREEN: You were talking a little bit about changing teacher education programs. Do you see a need for more discussion of this reflective practitioner role?

REGIE: I think university classes need to be conducted like whole language classrooms. You cannot have a university professor lecturing to university students and assigning texts and then expect these students to go into a classroom and give their students choices. The model has to change at the university level. You can't train teachers in methodology. They've got to see the model.

MAUREEN: What about teachers' writing?

REGIE: That's a good question. . . . But no, teachers don't write.

MAUREEN: Why not? Is it time? Is it fear?

REGIE: The way we were brought up. Teachers bought into Donald Graves's writing process, but what they do—I mean, many of them abort it. If they don't write themselves, then they take kids through all these steps. And I don't mean this as a criticism of teachers because I've done the same thing myself. I can remember, when his book first came out, going into a classroom and listing the steps of the writing process.

So I started there too, and I think it was only when I started writing myself that I realized that it just doesn't work like that. I try very hard when I'm working with teachers to do a lot of demonstration writing myself, and one of the things I've just started doing is even writing when I do a presentation, even if it's just a one-hour presentation, writing in front of teachers. And the room goes silent. I've had some teachers tell me they've never seen another teacher write. Most of us don't write.

MAUREEN: It's sad.

REGIE: Yes, but if we're talking about real, real is that most teachers don't write. And it's not because they don't want to. We're frozen with fear, based on the way most of us were taught to write, which was very mechanical. Most of us have not had extensive training in writing. I know very few teachers that have been through a writing project, that have been immersed the way I was in the National Writing Project, for example.

MAUREEN: Do you feel that's necessary?

REGIE: I do. . . . I have been astounded at the power of the written word. I don't see myself as a remarkable teacher. I see myself as a very conscientious, reflective teacher who has taken the time to write down what I've observed. But there are many, many teachers that are, I'm sure, more gifted and talented than I am. And I think the reason that I've been able to help teachers make their own changes is that I wrote my observations down.

The written word is powerful, and teachers should try to write an article, send it to a journal, and believe that what they have to say is important. . . . I think there have to be more people like myself, ordinary teachers, okay, conscientious teachers that are talking to other teachers.

MAUREEN: You wrote in *Transitions* that every teacher should have a personal educational philosophy, and you urge teachers to continue questioning how and why we do what we do. Are most teachers open to this?

REGIE: After a while. I think that what we found, for instance, in our support groups, was that nobody wanted to deal with theory the first year. And that's not because we're not conscientious and hardworking—I think it's often misinterpreted. It's because the management had to get in place.

MAUREEN: Classroom management?

REGIE: Yes, and once that was in place, once the teachers had some activities, some of the questions, some of the different ways they were going to handle using literature, then they could start to reflect. But I don't think you can reflect when you're very busy just with nuts and bolts. . . . I think you've got to have a certain amount of organization and management in place before you can do that reflection.

In order for teachers to sit back and observe what's going on, in order to take anecdotal records, in order to look at a literature discussion group and make some notes and see who's interacting with whom, who's taking the lead in what's happening—that's very sophisticated—that requires such good organization and management and cooperative learning and collaboration, and that doesn't just happen. It takes a long time to get to that point.

MAUREEN: Was it hard for you to write your own theory of learning in *Invitations*?

REGIE: Very hard. I wrote down my beliefs about evaluation, and I wrote down my beliefs about staff development. I wrote it as a way for teachers to reflect on their own [beliefs], but it's difficult to do.

We haven't taken the time as teachers to say, "This is what I value." For example, if we're teaching reading: "I value that kids are choosing their own books"; "I value that they're involved in literature discussion"; or "I value that they're keeping a record of books read." What is it that you value? Initially teachers didn't want to take time for that. They wanted answers.

MAUREEN: So how do you cope with that?

REGIE: You have to give them some answers. One of the things I do when I do a workshop is that I give them a lot of theory, but I always give them a lot of practice. I'll show them how you can teach a skill from the literature. I will demonstrate how you can teach phonics from a book and how and when and why I do it. I'll take them through the steps.

But at the same time, I'll give them the theory. And they'll listen to the theory because the practice is there, too. I think the whole notion of theory and practice going together is just so important. . . . The way it has to work is that evaluation and theory just become a part of teaching. But I think it takes a long time to get there.

MAUREEN: What do you say to teachers when they are faced with some new research or new methods, teachers who might say, "Gee, do you mean everything I've done up to this point has been wrong?"

REGIE: I think the one thing about whole language that has been so wonderful is that you start with strengths. You look at the child, and you say, "This is what he does; this is what he can do."

We have to do the same thing for us. I say to the teacher, "Look at what you're already doing. Literally pat yourself on the back. You're already reading aloud to children. You've been doing that for years. You do sustained silent reading; you're giving kids some choice in their topics of writing. So let's look at what we are doing and start with that." I always start right there.

But administrators, if they're not well-educated, expect this kind of change to happen very quickly. They want results fast. And this is not a quick fix. It takes a long time. We all have to be patient. It's like gardening.

MAUREEN: How?

REGIE: You can nurture it, and you can support it, and yet, these plants are going to take off in their own direction, to some degree, no matter what you do. And every year it's going to be a little bit different. And every year I change something, and I move something in the garden, just as I move something in my classroom.

I might have these wonderful plans of exactly how I want this, but when it actually comes out, it's never perfect, which is, I guess, some of the beauty of it. And there are lots of surprises, and there's always more work to be done. You're never there. I've never heard anybody say, "My garden is perfect this year. It's exactly the way I want it."

And I think that's really true with teaching, if you're a teacher-researcher, and you're looking at your teaching. . . . I'm really proud of the two books I've written, but I don't think they're "the answers." There's just so much more to learn.

I'm always looking around at my garden and thinking, like I'm looking at this clematis coming up and I'm thinking, "Gee, I think I want to put either another color clematis here or I want to try it this way, 'cause, yes, this looks nice, but I think it could look even better." I'd like to change it, just a little bit. Even the way the sun comes in is different because of the way we've got these huge trees and the way they shade our house.

And my frustration is that I can't get these roses to grow because we don't have enough sun. And yet, I keep planting roses. I get one beautiful rose—look behind you.

MAUREEN: Oh, I see!

REGIE: There's this gorgeous pink rose here, and there's this beautiful white rose here, but it's not a proliferation of roses. And yet, I'll take that, because it's still—it's beautiful. You know, I haven't given up on it. And I think that's what good teachers do, they never give up.

References

Routman, Regie. 1991. *Invitations: Changing as Teachers and Learners, K through 12*. Portsmouth, NH: Heinemann.

———. 1988. *Transitions: From Literature to Literacy*. Portsmouth, NH: Heinemann.

CURIOSITY IN THE CLASSROOM

BONI GRAVELLE
Iolani School
Honolulu, Hawaii

*U*ntil this year it didn't even occur to me that I could or should do research. I am a teacher. I've been one for more than two decades. In my interpretation, "researchers" were most often found at the university level or were those who got a Masters or Doctorate—and definitely were higher up in the educational hierarchy than I. Do you sense my feeling of inadequacy? Good.

At one time I thought I was the only classroom teacher intimidated by "experts" who gathered and interpreted research and then reported to us their knowledge of educational methods, philosophy, and the implied-direction that we should take. Recently, however, I was reading Bill Moyer's interview of a teacher, Mike Rose, and Rose spent a great deal of time discussing how uncomfortable he felt being interviewed, citing a "sort of nagging doubt that [he] had a right to speak" as an expert (Moyers 1990, p. 219).

MOYERS: What does that say about the mystique of education in this country? That somehow, even after twenty years of teaching street kids, slum kids, illiterate adults, people who can't get out of the neighborhoods, the lost people of our society, that you don't take yourself quite seriously as a competent authority?

ROSE: Interesting, isn't it? The raw power of education, particularly higher education, is so strong, I think, that it can act to deny our most immediate and true experience (Moyers 1990, p. 219).

Bingo. There was my interpretation of myself being echoed by *someone else*. In speaking with my colleagues, I found that many of us feel this distance between ourselves and the experts, who are frequently researchers. Writing this article for *Workshop* took on new meaning for me, because I realized that in order to be effective and innovative teachers, we first must give ourselves a lot more credit than we now do. I was wrong to see university professors as the only experts and the only researchers. Such a perception hinders us from using research as a very valuable tool to help us evaluate what is happening in our classrooms.

Iolani School—the K–12 private school in Honolulu, Hawaii where I teach—provided an opportunity for me to change my self-perception. In 1965, Harold Keables, a dynamic and demanding English teacher, came to teach at Iolani School after reaching retirement age. He showed his students the wonders of writing and led them to achievements in their writing that they had never dreamed themselves capable of. To honor him after his death, the Harold Keables Chair was founded. The money has been used each year to bring "experts in writing" to our school to act as visiting professors for a week and enable both students and teachers to rub elbows with "real" writers.

The wrong experts, I realized upon reflection, could possibly widen the gap . . . making us more in awe of them and less in awe of ourselves. In order to benefit from an expert by learning from one, we really needed to believe that we, too, are "experts." Last year, Thomas Newkirk, director of the New Hampshire Writing Program, was selected to visit the lower school. More than one of us was wary as we awaited the arrival of Dr. Newkirk. Tom, however, was a perfect choice. He viewed his stay as a "celebration of writing" and, with that as a basis, we all quickly and gratefully felt at ease to share and exchange ideas as colleagues. Instead of losing time bridging the gap in our expertise, we spent our time sharing, talking, questioning, and listening. In effect, he made us more, rather than less, confident about our abilities as teachers of writing.

Dr. Newkirk gave weight to the value of our ideas. As a result, and after delving into some of his research (Newkirk 1989), I got braver and started a form of recorded "research" of my own for my own information. Now I am aware that I can be a researcher, although neither to receive a degree (the reason I would have done research before) nor for statistics to prove or disprove my "theories." Since my purpose differs from most researchers', I don't feel the need to be as exacting as scholars. I am researching for myself out of curiosity to try to make sense out of what my students are doing and to be more aware of what is happening in my classroom. I use the information *to reflect* on what has happened, *to evaluate and assess* my progress, *to create* new avenues that will enable each child to feel successful as a writer, and *to invent* record-keeping methods that meet my needs.

Reflection can be disturbing. Looking into a mirror that might show us our faults as teachers isn't always easy. I remember my excitement at hearing from the experts that "every child had stories to tell" as the doors opened into the whole language movement. The days of regimented, boring writing assignments were coming to an end in the lower grades and there was promise of a joy in writing. But before long I realized that I couldn't get all of my students to tell the stories that they *must* have in their heads. The experts knew how to get these stories down on paper, but I didn't. I was almost afraid to confide to anyone my failure to elicit the stories from my students. Not only did I feel I was a failure, but the gap between the experts and me, as a classroom teacher, grew wider. I had to do a lot of serious thinking. It was this reflection that allowed me to see where I was having trouble. In order to give value to my thoughts, I had to have more confidence in myself, rather than just accepting what the experts were saying.

I then realized that I agreed: every child can write, although not every child has stories to tell. The key word for me, *stories*, or my interpretation of the word, was limiting possibilities for success. Stories are usually narratives and not all children can come up with a narrative that they feel good about. Some children soon sense that others do it more effortlessly, more quickly, and end up with a more pleasing result. While we may eventually be able to change the perception of these children and get them to the point where they are wonderful storytellers, I needed to take another path in the meantime.

Just as I was insecure about my ability to be a contributor to the teaching techniques of writing instruction, some children doubt their abilities or talents as writers. Although they may all be able to write, they truly have to realize and believe that fact. Confidence is the key. After realizing how difficult it was for me to believe in myself, I better understood how children might struggle to become confident in themselves. As a result, my task became to help the children find some form of writing that would make them perceive themselves as competent writers. By using more variety in my writing activities, I believed I would discover areas, other than "stories," where my young writers could excel.

Not only do I tell children early in the year that they have stories to tell, but I also tell them there are many ways of writing that we will explore as a class. I add that they can expect to feel successful with a number of them, though possibly not all. Some methods may be easier or more challenging for different individuals. But by trying out many forms of writing we will all find something that we are particularly fond of. Now we feel like we're off on an adventure, and tomorrow's activity may just convince one more of my students that he or she really is a writer!

In the past my writing activities, though varied in topic, were just too similar in format. I needed to get out of my rut of journals and pages of newsprint stapled together as my predominant repository of "children's stories." I'm sure this ho-hum similarity stifled some children's enthusiasm for writing. Now I'm constantly seeking simple formats based on simple ideas that accomplish perhaps the hardest task we face: making each child believe that he or she is a successful writer.

I am also developing record-keeping forms that can easily be filled out with information that allows me to track every student's progress. One form I created listed various reasons for writing: this insured that I had provided a variety of activities and also pointed out to me which type of writing each child felt better about. After tracking a sampling of Blake's work (figure 1), I begin to get an idea of the types of writing he enjoys and does well. I pull those selections from his writing folder and praise him using the information recorded on this form. I don't imply to him that this is the only type of writing he does well, but rather use this information to increase his overall confidence.

Nicky, another previously reluctant writer, put a lot more effort in his writing after such a conference. I received just the reinforcement I was looking for in a note that appeared on my desk. "Dear misis Gorvell I No I Riit a Lot Beekus I Like to Riit a Lot Love Nicky." I jotted this milestone down on Nicky's chart and glued his special note to the outside of his writing folder. By using more varied projects and assessing them fairly quickly and easily with the input on the forms, I found myself much more aware of the progress the children and I were making.

Riddles and poems are some of the simpler, and sometimes more successful, activities we pursue. Here is one of my favorite

Figure 1   Excerpt from Blake's record-keeping form

Name **Blake**   Evaluation of different types of writing

A- to get things done   E-to explain to others
B-for interpersonal relations   F-to re-create past events
C-to solve problems   G-poetry
D-to pretend and imagine   H-other

Code	Assignment	Date	Content	Effort	Art	Skills	Comments
D	letter to leprechaun	3/12/90	great! O lots of ques-tions sounds "real"	great voc. O centipedes poison	n/a	used ? mixes cap. and lower case	understands tricks keeps explains play
E	Say-Never Say chose "elephant"	3/21/91	fair- S got a little off-track	enjoyed S+ doing this paper.	cute elephant, even upside down	work on writing in straighter lines- hard to follow	

examples of *parts of a whole*: "A tail is part of a dog. A hop is part of a frog." This section's approach is right up a kindergartner's alley. One child comes up with a word like *bee* and, if the child needed help, the class would suggest parts of a bee. Timmy, often a noncontributor in large group discussions, proudly offered "a stinger is part of a bee" (figure 2). He was able to say this boldly because of the input from his classmates. We'd then find a word that rhymed with *bee*, like *tree*. Another child supplied "A leaf is part of a tree." Each child then illustrated his or her contribution and soon we had a beautiful twenty-four-page book, one page for each child, with terrific lessons on parts of a whole. More importantly, I had picked up quite a few children who began to think, "I can do this. I can write!" We were also lucky enough to have a wonderful seventy-year-old deaf woman come to our class and teach us how to "sign" this book. We dedicated this book to her and made her a copy. I'm not sure who was more pleased!

Another simple idea that fosters participation uses the pattern of a poem. One of my favorites is based on the last two lines of a marvelous poem by Beverly McLoughland from *Cricket* called "How to Talk to Your Snowman" (1990). It describes what you can say to a snowman, like "freezing and snow," but the last line admonishes, "But whatever you never say, never say: *bake*." The class again brainstormed "cold" words (ice cream, igloo, penguin) and "hot" words (fire, hot, toaster). After making torn construc-

Figure 2   Timmy's contribution to Parts of a bee *activity*

A stinger is part of a bee by Timmy

tion-paper snowmen and adding snow (we put white paint on screening and then blew), each child completed the sentence "never say _____, but you can try _____ or say _____." Erin's choices of "matches" and "popsicle and snowskating" made her feel very successful (figure 3). Each child was able to come up with unique ideas, even though some children took longer than others. As a result, a few more children began to feel good about writing.

I was reinforcing my belief that attitude or confidence was just as important as innate ability, and this was an area that I previously hadn't been working on hard enough. I will continue to test my hypothesis that the more variety I use in my writing activities, the sooner I will find the one activity that convinces one more child that he or she can write. To help children who were just beginning to believe in themselves, I found that doing a similar, although not repetitive task, was very beneficial. For example, a week after the snowman activity, a follow-up activity (they chose their own subject) was done much more easily, and, for some, in greater depth. Kelley wrote: *"Mom. Say I love you. Never say I hate you Mom. I wish you wrnt my mom."*

Another way I evaluated my students' writing was by using another form (figure 4), in reference to Mark's personalized ending to the story *The Snowy Day* by Ezra Jack Keats (1962)

Figure 3   Erin's choices for "cold" words

(figure 5). I easily filled out column D in the chart (figure 4). If I thought a comment was warranted, I would write it in the corresponding space at the bottom. For this particular assignment I wrote in spaces 1 (content), 4 (neatness), and 8 (creativity). Although we don't grade students on their writing at this level, the form was valuable in helping me become more aware of individual strengths and weaknesses. In addition, it also showed me when there was growth in their confidence. The checkmarks kept me posted on their progress and the comments helped me recall specific areas in more detail. In addition, at the top of this

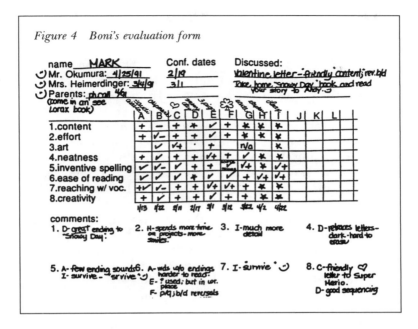

Figure 4   Boni's evaluation form

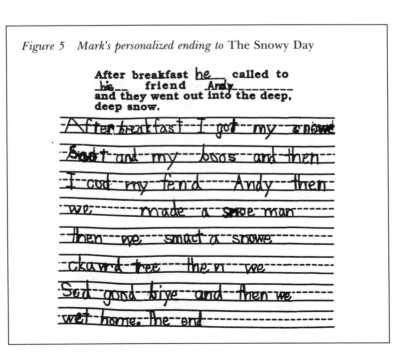

Figure 5   Mark's personalized ending to The Snowy Day

sheet I write the names of our principal, the head of our language arts department, and the child's parents. I like to bolster the child's ego by sending each child to these administrators and by notifying the parents of "special" work. This form helps me follow through on these important confidence builders. The top right-hand side is used to record notes from teacher-child conferences.

I am also very curious about two aspects of inventive spelling. First, how effective was this technique with my students? I knew that after reading their writing over a period of time I was able to decipher most of the writing quite easily. I was a "safe" reader for them. Unfortunately, I wasn't always able to have every child read to me immediately after they had written. With some very young writers, unless you got to them right away, they couldn't remember what they had said. I found this to be a hard thing for some of them, and even me, to handle. As a result, it was a real confidence loser, something I desperately wanted to avoid. To become more familiar with each child's style of inventive spelling, I began selecting some of the simpler activities, where the amount of writing was limited, and then wrote down the words they had spelled correctly and the words they had written inventively. Figure 6 shows the information I recorded from Jamie's letter to the sow after hearing James Marshall's *The Three Little Pigs* (1989). It was very eye-opening for me to see how well the children were doing. But even with those who weren't close to the actual spellings, this research taught me a lot. For example, I soon realized the phonics skills that a group of children were ready to be taught, although the *dr* and *gr* sounds were glaringly hard for some of my students to determine. I also became more aware of certain children "hearing" sounds wrong in their heads or applying their speech deficiencies to their writing.

Secondly, I also was curious about whether or not children could or would read each other's work if it was written with inventive spelling. Children's printing (reversals such as *b/d* and *p/q* can really throw you off, as in "bo" for "do") and "sounding out" interpretations (*apos* and *apls* for *apples*) were often different and at times challenging. How could I get my five-and six-year olds to read and enjoy each other's work in such books as our *How to Talk to Your Snowman*? If I corrected their spelling or wrote the correct spelling on their page, would their feelings be hurt and cause them to lack confidence in their ability to spell? Tom Newkirk and I discussed this and we wondered if children

Figure 6   Jamie's Invented Spelling Evaluation

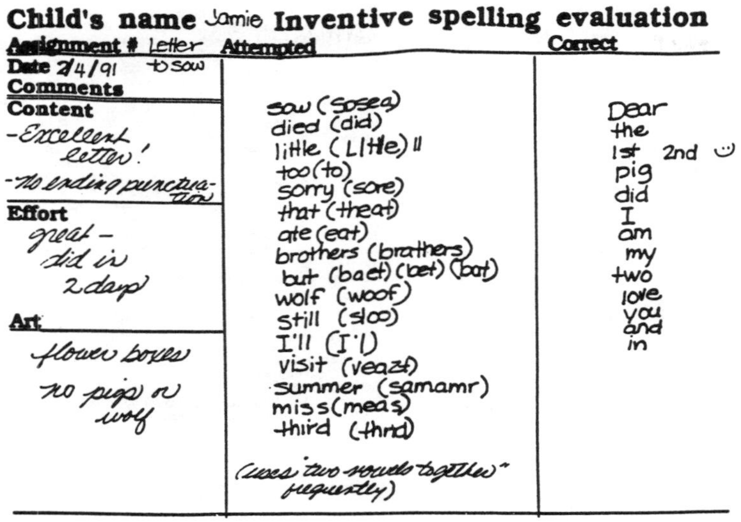

Child's name Jamie **Inventive spelling evaluation**

Assignment # letter   Attempted   Correct

Date 2/4/91   to sow

Comments

Content

- *Excellent letter!*

- *no ending punctuation*

Effort

great –
did in
2 days

Art

flower boxes

no pigs n wolf

Attempted	Correct
sow (sosea)	Dear
died (did)	the
little (LItte) !!	1st 2nd ☺
too (to)	pig
sorry (sore)	did
that (theat)	I
ate (eat)	am
brothers (brathers)	my
but (baet) (bet) (bat)	two
wolf (woof)	love
still (sloo)	you
I'll (I'l)	and
visit (veazs)	in
summer (samamr)	
miss (meas)	
third (thrd)	
(uses two sounds together frequently)	

were really interested in reading the other children's writing or only interested in reading their own, which they *could* decipher. The awareness of this as a concern led me, when time allowed, to try something new. Our *Honest, It's Abe*! book culminated our study of Lincoln. Each child illustrated and wrote a page based on what they remembered about Lincoln. Out of curiosity, I typed all of the children's contributions correctly on one sheet along with their names and placed it at the back of the book (figure 7).

After reading *The Jacket I Wear in the Snow* by Shirley Neitzel (1989) as part of our snow unit, the children dressed a paper-doll-like drawing in winter clothing (a challenging concept when you live in Hawaii!) using construction-paper scraps. They then completed the following form: "This is the _____, all _____ and _____, that I wear in the snow" (figure 8). Again, at the end of the book, the children's responses were spelled correctly. I put them at the end to downplay the importance of correct spelling, so that the children would know I was sincerely pleased with their attempts at sounding out the

Figure 7   Student's contribution on Abraham Lincoln

Ryan	Abraham Lincoln was a nice man.
Brendan	Abraham Lincoln's birthday is today.
Tim	Abraham Lincoln was nice to lots of us.
Nicky	Abraham Lincoln was funny.
Megan	Abraham Lincoln was helpful.
Jason	Abraham Lincoln's father was a carpenter.
Karen	Abraham Lincoln was always honest.
Mark	Abraham Lincoln freed the black people.
Emily	Abraham Lincoln always read lots of books so he could be a good reader and so he could be a smart man.
Brent	Abraham Lincoln was a kind person that helped people like the prisoners. He cut down trees. He was wise too.
Jamie	Abraham Lincoln was a lawyer.
Jackie	Abraham Lincoln had a home.
Kelley	Abraham Lincoln was the 16th president.
Jayna	Abraham Lincoln told good stories.
Karlyn	Abraham Lincoln loved to read and write.
Ross	Abraham Lincoln got shot when he was watching a movie.
Erin	Abraham Lincoln had a family.
Misha	Abraham Lincoln got to be a president. May 14.
Maridith	Abraham Lincoln is kind because everybody liked Abraham Lincoln.
Kristen	Abraham Lincoln's mother died.
Sean	Abraham Lincoln was a good man.
Gage	Abraham Lincoln was a good president.
Blake	Abraham Lincoln was nice.

words they wanted to use. I explained, however, to the children that this was the "universal spelling" of the words they had used and that I could send our book far away and those people who weren't clever at reading children's writing could use that page to help them understand our class's writing style. I felt this technique did serve its purpose, for a few children eagerly read the books we had published, even though at times they only read a few words or pages. They were making an attempt to read each others' writing, although more so at the end of the year when their reading skills were more developed and they were more confident readers. I also liked having the universal spellings because parents could use it to read their child's writing without implying to the child that what was written was too difficult for them to decode, another confidence-builder.

In other classroom books, such as our *A Child Is Part of a Kindergarten*, I had the children copy and correctly spell what they had dictated to me (figure 2). Given the choice, the children tended to read these books more than the ones using inventive spelling, although I realize there are many factors involved in their choices—the content, the art, and so forth. I am curious about what I can do to make the books using inventive spelling more reader-friendly. I'd like to devise a method that both reinforces inventive spelling and makes the children's wonderful

Figure 8   Ross's paper doll

This is the _Big Ross_____.
all_ichiy___and__Worm__.
that I wear in the snow

name ROSS

writing available to a wider audience that uses a minimum amount of teacher time. Now that ought to be challenging!

Although I have neither the time to devote to a comprehensive study, nor an assistant to hand the task to, the record-keeping techniques that I have developed have been fairly quick and easy to fill out and it has been time well-spent. By using the information gathered, I am learning a great deal about my teaching and I am much more aware of which skills are sinking in and being applied. I see growth in my students' ability and desire to express themselves.

Perhaps the greatest value in this issue of *Workshop* lies not in the research ideas or techniques presented, but in the awareness that we, too, can be effective researchers. We also need to believe in ourselves and realize that we have more potential than we thought. Somehow I sense that Harold Keables is nodding his head in agreement.

References

Keats, Ezra Jack. 1962. *The Snowy Day*. New York: The Viking Press.

Marshall, James. 1989. *The Three Little Pigs*. New York: Dial Books.

McLoughland, Beverly. 1990. "How to Talk to Your Snowman." *Cricket* (January).

Moyers, Bill. 1990. *A World of Ideas II: Public Opinions from Private Citizens*. New York: Doubleday.

Neitzel, Shirley. 1989. *The Jacket I Wear in the Snow*. New York: Scholastic.

Newkirk, Thomas. 1989. *More Than Stories: The Range of Children's Writing*. Portsmouth, NH: Heinemann.

DREAMING AWAY: ADVENTURES IN NONFICTION

TIM HILLMER
Choice Program
Platt Middle School
Boulder, Colorado

*O*n the first day of school last year, I watched the seventh graders as they arrived in my room and were drawn instantly to the class library. I was hoping to surprise even the most avid readers with Cynthia Voight's latest offering or Avi's new thriller, and had spent part of my summer buying books so that the library would be well-stocked with short story anthologies, contemporary dramas, mystery books, science fiction and fantasy novels, as well as poetry collections. The students clustered in front of the shelves and examined covers, made recommendations to friends, and asked the inevitable question: "Can we check out more than one?"

But not everyone was so excited. A handful of boys perused the titles with sour looks on their faces, then walked coldly away without even picking up a book. They returned to their desks to examine a science or math or social studies textbook. How could they be so disinterested? How could they *not* be thrilled? I later learned that they were all brilliant students with especially strong interests in science and math. Nicknamed the "little professors" by a colleague, they'd won numerous awards in the Quiz Bowl, science fair, and Mathcounts competitions.

I was persistent with these boys. Throughout the year I gently recommended an assortment of intriguing fiction. They'd usually take the books home, perhaps out of kindness to me, then return them unread the following day. One student spent part of the year reading a scientific account of Admiral Peary's arctic adventures. The others browsed through wholesale computer catalogs and science magazines. They hardly touched any literary

65

fiction unless it was assigned. When the school year ended, I felt
a deep sense of frustration and failure that I'd never motivated
them as readers.

I remained puzzled about how to deal with students like the
"little professors" until the following summer when I took a class
in composition research and theory at the University of New
Hampshire. One of our individual projects was to conduct an
interview on some aspect of a person's literacy. I decided to
interview Margery Milne, a retired University of New Hampshire professor, who had a lifetime of literacy on which to reflect.
Ms. Milne was a renowned author and naturalist who, along with
her husband, Lorus J. Milne, had written nearly fifty books on
natural history subjects. She'd conducted field studies throughout North and South America, Panama, the West Indies, Europe,
Africa, Asia, Australia, New Zealand, the South Pacific, Hawaii,
and the Galapagos Islands. She had also worked on assignment
for *National Geographic* and other magazines, and her travels
were documented in two television shows: "Bold Journey" and
"I Search For Adventure."

Ms. Milne was a joy to interview. She was a peppy, boisterous
woman who seemed younger than her sixty-plus years might
indicate. Her sentences were rapid-fire and sprinkled with laugh-
ter and colorful phrases like "Oh boy!" and "Amazing!"
Throughout the interview I was continually impressed by her
energy and enthusiasm in the areas of biology, natural history,
and ecology.

I'd carefully organized my questions beforehand so I could
tape-record information about her favorite authors, as well as
her earliest memories as a reader and writer. But midway
through the interview, I decided to ask a different kind of question: "What don't you like to read?"

"Well, I used to read novels," she said, "but I don't read them
anymore."

Surprised, I asked, "Why not?"

"It seems like a waste of time," she said. "I'm not reading
anything I can use. On the other hand, if I'm reading nonfiction,
then it might be something I could use in my teaching and
writing. Or if I read things in natural history and science and
ecology and it's got a lot of nature in it, then I might be able to
use that. I'd rather spend my time reading stuff like that than
novels. I mean I like facts. I want facts. I used to read nonfact
novels, but now I don't waste my time. It's ridiculous."

Being an avid reader of fiction, I was shocked and puzzled.

When I told her of my reaction, she let out a hearty laugh and said, "You're just *dreaming away* in novels." This exchange fascinated me. How could someone consider reading fiction a waste of time?

But there was a familiar ring to her response. I thought of the "little professors" and their "antifiction" reading habits, then made a connection with my own reading tastes and how they might have influenced the way I selected books and literature for the classroom. I've always had a deep love for fiction, but tend to avoid nonfiction, especially any titles that deal with science and math, which were my worst subjects in school. I realized that my selections for the class library may have been swayed by my own reading interests. In the past, I'd often rationalized a fiction focus because I felt students received enough technical reading in their science and math classes. It was my duty to expose them to literature, namely fictional materials that could help their imaginations take flight.

Later in the interview, I made another important connection. When I asked Ms. Milne about the writers she'd read and admired, she talked of her experiences as a young girl visiting the American Museum of Natural History. "I'd sneak into the staff library where I wasn't allowed just so I could browse through the natural history books. That was all that interested me. I'd read the stories of the great explorers. I'd certainly read Livingston, who went to Africa, along with some of the explorers from the American Museum of Natural History. They fascinated me and I always went to their lectures. I knew when I was ten-years-old that I wanted to be like them. And I remember Martin and Osa Johnson, the explorers who went to Africa in the early nineteen hundreds. I read the writers from the past. Darwin. All those old-timers and their books, some of them published in the eighteen hundreds."

When I asked her to elaborate on the contents of the books, she described them in an excited voice as being scientific journals of the author's research expeditions to exotic places. "That's what I loved to do," she said. "*Dream away* about all the adventures they went on and how I could do the same."

It wasn't until later, when I listened to the tape-recorded interview at home, that I realized Ms. Milne had just described nonfiction in exactly the same way she'd earlier described fiction: *dreaming away*. Perhaps these "stuffy" scientific journals and books were able to capture the same compelling literary themes as the fantasy and mystery novels I'd pushed at my science-oriented students all year. Perhaps the "little professors" could dream away while reading Darwin's account of his scientific adventures in the Galapagos, or Livingston's journeys across Africa. Perhaps I needed to create a special section in my classroom library that contained the literature of science and natural history.

When I asked Ms. Milne to talk about the role nonfiction can play in stimulating a reader's imagination and creativity, her answer was again a surprise, forcing me to reevaluate the process my students usually go through in researching information for a writing assignment.

"First," she said, "you need to get kids outdoors and in the field in order to observe things outside. Later have them read and recognize things and say 'That's what I saw!' and talk about it. I think you need to be outside observing things firsthand and using your senses. What are you smelling? What are you hearing? What's growing? Do the observation first, then read about it. It's more meaningful that way."

As a teacher, I'd always believed that the first step in gathering information about a topic of interest was to read, and then later pursue the topic in-depth through field trips and guest speakers. But what she had said made perfect sense, especially in the areas of natural history and science. "Get kids out first, get them excited, pay attention to certain things, then come back and read about it."

In his book *Investigate Nonfiction* (1989), Donald Graves writes about the importance of observation in a school project. "Direct observation is an important source of information. Our lives are filled with hundreds of processes occurring simultaneously at any given moment within a few feet of us" (p. 25). "Somewhere in the school yard or near it, mark off a piece of land with stakes. . . . The purpose of this longer-term data gathering project is to note the many kinds of change that occur on this one small piece of land over a year. The land does not have to be in the country. As long as there is something growing, even if it is only weeds, the project can be successful, since where there is life there will be change. . . . The *first* step is to see *what* is there. . . . *What is growing?* . . . . *What is moving?* . . . . *What are the effects of weather?*" [italics added] (pp. 29–30).

Milne and Graves made me think of my own classroom and a project I asked students to do which involved researching a variety of animals. In the past, our first step was to go to the library and begin reading and gathering information. Why not just reverse the process? We could first go to a zoo or a veterinarian's office or a wildlife refuge in order to observe animals in the field. Then, later, after the initial observation had taken place, we could return to the library and begin reading and writing. It all seemed so simple. Yet I would never have seen this unless I'd interviewed a trained naturalist like Ms. Milne who understood the importance of observation first, and reading and recognition second.

I learned a valuable lesson from Margery Milne about the literacy interests of young scientists. Strong readers may not always be motivated by dragons or mythical heroes or super detectives. Sometimes a student might be just as compelled to read "literature" by discovering the arctic beauty of the North Pole through the journals of Admiral Peary, then comparing this same region with a contemporary perspective that might be found in *National Geographic*.

I also realized that I don't always have the answers when it comes to understanding the individual needs of the students in my classroom. I'm often swayed by my own tastes and opinions, and may not have the expertise in art or science or history to challenge the literacy interests of all students. But, as Elliot Eisner discusses in his book *The Enlightened Eye* (1991), I do have the potential for *connoisseurship*: "The ability to make fine-grained discriminations among complex and subtle qualities is an instance of what I have called *connoisseurship*. Connoisseurship is the art of appreciation . . . (63). Connoisseurship is the means through which we come to know the complexities, nuances, and subtleties of aspects of the world in which we have a special interest" (68).

I do have the ability as a curious researcher to ask questions, to seek out information, and to invite historians, scientists, and artists into the school so that our classroom community can see through their eyes and begin to understand their unique visions.

Sometimes conducting research can take a fascinating, unexpected turn. I'd interviewed Ms. Milne intent on gathering information about her literacy development. Instead I discovered something about myself as a teacher and why my fiction-oriented approach with the "little professors" had failed. More importantly, she helped me to see clearly into the minds of the young scientists in my classroom, and showed me that careful observation is as essential to the world of the teacher as it is to the naturalist.

In the prologue to their book, *A World Alive: The Natural*

Wonders of a New England River Valley (1991), Lorus and Margery Milne wrote: "The world outside one's door is as fascinating a community as can be found. The commonplaces that everyone can see, whether trees or animals or fields or water denizens, provide a perennial joy and consolation" (p. 13).

The same principle holds true for the way I view my classroom: the students are as fascinating a community as can be found. The commonplaces that everyone can see, whether in art or science or math or history, provide a perennial joy and consolation.

References

Eisner, Elliot W. 1991. *The Enlightened Eye: Qualitative Inquiry and the Enhancement of Educational Practice*. New York: Macmillan.

Graves, Donald H. 1989. *Investigate Nonfiction*. Portsmouth, N H: Heinemann.

Milne, Lorus and Margery. 1991. *A World Alive: The Natural Wonders of a New England River Valley*. Camden, ME: Yankee Books.

Some titles by Lorus and Margery Milne:

Milne, Lorus and Margery. 1980. *Gadabouts & Stick-At-Homes: Wild Animals and Their Habitats*. San Francisco: Sierra Club Books.

———. 1982a. *Dreams of a Perfect Earth*. New York: Atheneum.

———. 1982b. *Nature's Clean Up Crew: The Burying Beetles*. New York: Dodd, Mead.

———. 1982c. *A Time To Be Born: An Almanac of Animal Courtship and Parenting*. San Francisco: Sierra Club Books.

———. 1983a. *The Audubon Society Book of Insects*. New York: Harry N. Abrams.

———. 1983b. *Nature's Great Carbon Cycle*. New York: Atheneum.

———. 1984. *The Mystery of the Bog Forest*. New York: Dodd, Mead.

———. 1987. *A Shovelful of Earth*. New York: Henry Holt.

———. 1988. *The Behavior and Learning of Animal Babies*. Chester, CT: Globe Pequot Press.

———. 1989. *Understanding Radioactivity*. New York: Atheneum.

———. 1991. *Insects and Spiders*. New York: Doubleday.

THE NEVER-ENDING EXPOSITION

SUSAN RAIVIO
Athey Creek Middle School
West Linn, Oregon

*M*ost of us have seen or heard about the movie series *The NeverEnding Story*, those wonderful adventure films about a young boy whose dreams never end, but take him to unknown lands. As we get immersed in this film, creativity and imagination draw us into endless magical worlds that simply set the stage for further adventure. So it is with the writing of Jessica, a talented, mature sixth grader who "likes stories that don't end—so others can finish it their way." Much to the frustration of her teacher, Mrs. T., Jessica just stops a story dead without offering the resolution expected by most readers. Talented writers like Jessica present a challenge to every teacher not only because they tackle knowledge and creativity from new perspectives but also because they stretch us as teachers to make room within the regular classroom for the guidance and nurturance of such development.

An above-average student attending a whole language–centered middle school in suburban Portland, Oregon, Jessica is guided through her assignments by Mrs. T., an experienced teacher whose classroom practice is based on the works of Nancy Atwell (1987) and Donald Graves (1983). She provides writing opportunities through modified workshops, which she mixes with traditional writing assignments to expose students to conventional writing genres.

In her fifteen years of teaching, Mrs. T. has never before felt the frustration she now does with Jessica. She perceives a great imbalance between Jessica's aptitude and ability and her writing style and attitude. Mrs. T's concerns lie in polishing Jessica's style and final product without squashing her creativity. Jessica's technique has also aroused Mrs. T.'s curiosity. Jessica is one of those children who loves to write creatively. She participated in extracurricular writer's workshops through much of her elementary school education. From these experiences, Jessica feels she is stimulated to explore new concepts in writing. These sessions afforded her the opportunity to hone her skills and test new styles.

"I'm a good writer," she states as a simple matter of fact. "I use good description and action and I make the reader think."

Her teacher agrees, but feels that this high self-regard might stand in Jessica's way of learning new styles and techniques of more conventional writing patterns.

"She never writes a conclusion. She needs polish," Mrs. T. comments to me.

Enter the Teacher-Researcher

Because of my discussions with Jessica and my frequent observations as a substitute teacher in this class, Jessica has put me in the role of writing mentor, the person off whom she bounces her ideas and writing strategies. I feel more like a negotiator. I hear both her ideas of style and concepts and her teacher's concerns about her work and expectations for class assignments. Both express hope that I can shed some light and propose a solution to the current dilemma: the never-ending exposition.

The Story of One Assignment

The class assignment is to write a story using the classic approach of exposition, rising action, climax, falling action, and resolution. Jessica appears to feel good about the task.

"I'll have to make it long to get all my words out."

She has trouble deciding whether to write a mystery, horror story, or a comedy.

"Well, I usually write comedies for laughs."

But the idea of a mystery or horror tale sounds intriguing.

"Yes, I like to make horror stories sound happy at the start— to make it seem weirder. Then I let it go scary. I usually make one person the mystery."

"Sounds like you have a scheme in mind already," I nudge a bit, trying to pin her down. She agrees.

Then she goes to her desk and sits, and sits some more. I

ignore her and pretend to observe others in the class. After a good twenty minutes I wander over to her desk.

"Jessica, what are you doing?"

"Thinking. I need a long time to get the game plan in my head, but I'm ready now."

And the writing begins—nose-to-the-grindstone writing. The exposition portion is due tomorrow and she writes steadily. The daydreaming, staring-off-into-space posture are all part of the process of outlining and brainstorming. I thought she was off-task but, instead, she has become mentally organized.

Two days later I see Jessica in the hall at school.

"Want to see my rough drafts?"

"Drafts?"

"Yea, I couldn't decide so I wrote two, but this is the one I'm going to use." Jessica hands me two of the story beginnings: one a comedy and the other a horror story, indicating her preference for the horror idea.

"I didn't like the comedy. This one is good."

"Why, Jessica?"

"Because it's weird. The reader can really imagine and it will be fun to write. It felt better. Besides, the other kids liked it best."

Good old peer pressure strikes again. In class that day, each student presented her story beginnings to some classmates. Jessica told me her friends overwhelmingly chose the horror beginning.

"What do you think about that, Jessica?"

"Oh, well, I'd better do this one because the readers will like it better. My friends can't wait for me to finish the story."

"Will you finish the other comedy story?"

"No. It's not that good . . . too silly . . . a little gross."

A day passes and I'm observing in Jessica's language arts class again. She sits casually: feet propped up, fidgeting with pencils and intently examining some minute paper on the bulletin board adjacent to her desk. The rest of the class is writing the body of the story but Jessica seems unfocused. She comes over to me.

"I just can't get the words to come. No motivation."

"Any ideas why?"

"Not in the mood, I guess. I'll have to write at home tonight. I can't be forced to write and create."

Mrs. T. gives us the go-ahead to talk outside the room. She seems to realize Jessica is at a standstill.

"What's the problem, Jessica?"

"I don't want to follow the pattern. I like my stories to just stop. Just think about the big picture of things. People should be able to imagine how they want stories to end. I want others to use their minds."

"Not everyone is as creative as you."

"But I'm trying to give them the chance to be more worldly in their interpretations."

"Do you have the expertise to do that?"

"I can suggest—force the issue."

"But you do have some guidelines for this assignment."

"I know."

I touch bases with Mrs. T. She's frustrated.

"I can't seem to guide Jessica, to get her to break this pattern. She can't seem to grasp the concept of completing a story. I've talked to her but she feels she doesn't want to be bound by convention. I'm trying to support her but I want her to grow, too. Her stories are great—so imaginative. I'm wondering if she just isn't capable of pulling it all together. I told her that. I'm not sure why I'm so bothered!"

The end of the week arrives and Jessica's story is ready to be turned in, all beautifully bound in a blue cover with yellow bindings of yarn. Each student in turn reads her story. Jessica's "Mirror, Mirror on the Wall" is full of description and surreal images. It is superior to most of those already read. The class listens intently as the tale unfolds.

Mirror, Mirror on the Wall

It was at the stroke of twelve when I awoke. As I went outside to go to the bathroom I was drowned with fog, and as I held my hand in front of my face I could hardly make out my five fingers. You see my family was quite poor so the only bathroom we had was an outhouse, so I was surprised to hear running water outside since the sink was inside.

I cautiously stepped into the outhouse. It appeared to be normal. As I closed the door a chill went up my back. When I was done I stepped out and noticed that about an arms length away was a small orange stream. As I observed the orange substance more closely I noticed that there was no bottom to it. It just looked like a mirror reflecting all the orange water.

I was so curious that I decided to follow further down the hill. At the bottom of the hill the stream went into a cave. I was frightened but I was excited to see where it went, so I followed it inside.

Then again I heard the sound of water but this time louder and as if it was crashing to the earth. At the end of the cave there was a light and every second I was getting closer to it.

Then as I took my next step I was standing at the end of the cave and standing in front of one of the most amazing orange waterfalls. Everything about it was picture perfect all except one thing, just as the water was about to hit the ground it vanished into mid-air. It was amazing. Slowly I edged towards the waterfall then when I was about a stones throw away I jumped under the falls. Even though the falls vanished before any orange water hit me I felt as though I was getting soaked. I looked at myself and I didn't appear to be wet. Then I looked around there were mirrors on either side and mirrors in front and behind me there was even a mirror below and then when I looked above me where the waterfall had been there was a mirror above me and the waterfall had disappeared. But I still heard the sound of crashing water.

Then she stops. The pregnant pause . . . but the story is over. We all seem to be waiting for more but that's it. Then the murmurs start. Some children can't figure out what's going on. Others are discussing possible outcomes and explanations. Jessica tunes in to this last group and, with a satisfied smile, takes her seat. Mrs. T. makes no comment other than to make eye contact with me.

Over the weekend the papers are formally evaluated. Jessica receives an *A-* with compliments on her descriptions. Concerns are raised about her content and resolution. Mrs. T. asks if Jessica would like to write a continuation of her story.

As part of the evaluation process on Monday, each writer is asked to critique her own paper according to a standardized writing assessment format. Each facet of the assessment is explained and each writer is asked to rate herself on a scale of one to five points, with five the highest score. Jessica generally scores herself as 4. Mrs. T. then asks each student to identify that part of the story which corresponds to the five parts of an expositive piece. Jessica can identify the exposition, the rising action, the climax, but she does not indicate any part as the falling action or resolution.

Then they break into groups for assessment. The majority of students feel Jessica should have provided more resolution, that the end was too sudden. Two people like the style and have endings to offer.

Jessica comments to me, "Well, two of them have the right idea. The others just couldn't expand enough."

Hundreds of questions pound through my head at our post-writing conference, but Jessica begins. "I got an *A-*. I'm surprised. Thought she'd flunk me!" We laugh.

"Why?"

"Not really. But I didn't provide an ending."

"Why not?"

"Because that's not how I write. There's got to be room for writers like, like Stacy [her classmate with a similar style]. But Mrs. T. knows that. She's a great teacher."

I have my say. "I think Mrs. T. is making room for you. You certainly got a good grade. She's encouraging you to go on, to expand. Maybe she needs to know you can do it even if you would prefer not to write that way."

Later that day, Jessica and her buddy Stacy come bouncing up to me.

"Guess what we're going to do?"

I give up quickly.

"We're going to write a great new story, complete with all that expositive stuff. First we'll tell her we have another story, we'll read it, and then we'll stop halfway through. When we see that look on her face, we'll read the rest. It will be radical!"

Jessica and her cohort went on to do just that. Mrs. T. was thrilled and felt she had experienced success by just planting the seeds and gently probing. Jessica was quite proud of herself. She even admitted to liking the idea of formulating a conclusion.

Jessica, Meet Bobbie Ann

Part of me just could not let Jessica continue writing her cliffhangers without being introduced to the stories of Bobbie Ann Mason, that wonderful southern writer often noted for her rather abrupt endings. I wanted Jessica to read a published author who fancies the same style as she if for no other reason than to confirm her aspirations.

I gave Jessica a copy of "Shiloh," the saga of Norma Jean and LeRoy, whose marriage has soured (Mason 1990, pp. 219–33). In the story, Norma Jean's disillusionment with her spouse is as evident as LeRoy's enchantment with his wife of many years. At the end of the tale, the couple is at a park and Norma Jean, depressed, suspiciously heads toward the bluffs of the Tennessee River. And so the story ends.

Jessica's reaction to "Shiloh" was both revealing and confusing. At first, Jessica was angry that there was no completed resolution to the plot. When I mentioned that that is how she herself likes to write, she modified her tone and suggested that the author would be glad to have provoked a strong emotion. After she digested the fact that there was not a decisive resolution to the story, Jessica became excited that "A real-life published author could really end stories this way."

Jessica then commented that Mason was a great writer, an inspiration. In her opinion her own creative juices and emotions were stimulated; therefore, the author was a success. She liked the way Mason eases out of the story yet accomplishes what Jessica classified as real style and technique. It's something new for her to try.

Postscript

Jessica has since shared with me several ideas for stories and for the continuation of "Mirror, Mirror on the Wall." She uses the term "continuation." I see her ideas as resolutions with an open end, a compromise. But who am I to contradict her terms? For all I know, Jessica may write the *NeverEnding Story, Part III* and be recognized as a famous Hollywood playwright!

References

Atwell, Nancie. 1987. *In the Middle: Writing, Reading and Learning with Adolescents.* Portsmouth, NH: Heinemann.

Graves, Donald. 1983. *Writing: Teachers and children at work.* Portsmouth, NH: Heinemann.

Mason, Bobbie Ann. 1990. "Shiloh." In *We Are the Stories We Tell.* Toronto, Canada: Random House.

ASK THEM

KATHLEEN A. MOORE
Thorncliffe Elementary School
Toronto, Ontario

*E*valuation is inevitable. Whether we want it or plan for it, evaluation occurs in our classrooms. From the first day of September, my grade-three students observe their own and their fellow students' work to make comparisons. Teachers begin evaluating their students as soon as the new class lists are available. They scan their students' lists for bright lights or potential problems. Evaluation is built into the system of education. It's in our blood. Yet we seldom consult the central participants who can be lost in the mist of grades and numbers that swirl around their names. I have come to believe that "If a child is going to control and direct his own thinking . . . he must become conscious of it" (Donaldson 1978, p. 96).

In preparation for completing my grade-three class's achievement forms for June, I organized an occasion for my students to tell me what they had learned about writing and reading. I knew that evaluation took place daily and was a part of every interaction that went on in my classroom. Because so much of my teaching day was spent in observing and conferencing with my students, I felt confident of my knowledge of their progress. However, I wanted my students to be active participants in the evaluation process just as they had been involved in every phase of my planning, teaching, and assessment of the year's language program. I needed to hear the students articulate their own progress, and the students themselves needed the opportunity to reflect on their changes, growth, and accomplishments. I decided to interview my students.

I explained to the class that I would be interviewing each student and that there would be time for them to prepare what they wanted to tell me. I wrote the three questions I would ask on the blackboard: What have you learned about writing? What have you learned about reading? What do you plan to do next in writing and reading? I then gave my students time to peruse the contents of their writing folders and reading journals, time to reflect on the changes they could see, and time to prepare to talk with me about what they found.

I watched while my students went first to their writing folders. They read the stories they had written in September, their published books, and their most recent stories. They next organized their reading journals, and compared their September responses to their most recent entries. I could see them making discoveries about what they had learned and how they had changed. Finally, they began to formulate their future plans for their writing and reading. Some students were ready to be interviewed that same day. Others needed more time.

I interviewed all twenty-four students. I wrote every word the students said and when my scribbling lagged too far behind, they stopped, waited for me to catch up, and then proceeded without dropping a stitch. If we were interrupted, they were able to continue from where they had stopped without cues from me. In addition to the three main questions, I occasionally encouraged them to clarify their initial comments. Most of the time, all I needed to do was to wait with my pen poised over my page while they reported the progress they believed they had made in writing and reading. At the end of each interview, I read aloud to each student what he or she had said to make sure that I had recorded their thoughts correctly. I also pointed to the space remaining on the page where I had finished writing and said, "This is your space. If you think of anything you want me to add, let me know." Several did take advantage of this opportunity.

Saleena's Interview

Saleena is a small nine-year-old with a long, dark braid down her back and curling tendrils of hair around her face. She came to the interview with her writing folder and her reading journals but she did not need to refer to them. She answered my questions with little hesitation. Her voice was clear and firm. She was eager to explain and delighted to give examples of what she meant. She sat beside my desk with her back straight, not at all nervous. She looked at me waiting for me to ask the first question.

KATHLEEN: What have you learned about writing?

SALEENA: Before, I used to write stories like lists but now I know you should tell more.

KATHLEEN: Can you give me an example?

SALEENA: In my story about my brother, I wrote that sometimes I get really, really mad at him and I start screaming all over the place but sometimes I feel like I never want him to leave me.

KATHLEEN: How did you learn that?

SALEENA: If I listen to a story that's a list, I don't learn anything.

KATHLEEN: What else have you learned about writing?

SALEENA: I didn't know how to write in September. I didn't know that my reading would help my writing. I thought reading was just reading and not ideas.

KATHLEEN: Can you give an example?

SALEENA: Like the book, *Dreams of Victory* [(Conford 1973)]. She has a problem. She didn't tell anyone. She tried to solve it in her dreams. That's unusual.

KATHLEEN: Anything else?

SALEENA: In September, I was writing about plans to go somewhere. Now I realize I could have written in chapters. They start a whole new thing. When you want to switch to a new topic, you can begin a new chapter.

KATHLEEN: How did you learn that?

SALEENA: Hussain's story about his birthday gave me that idea. I also learned other stuff from listening to the other kids' stories. Especially Reshma. I like all her stories.

KATHLEEN: Anything else?

SALEENA: I learned about where to put commas and quotation marks.

KATHLEEN: How did you learn that?

SALEENA: By reading.

KATHLEEN: What have you learned about reading?

SALEENA: In reading, I realize that I understand more words than in September and that I can figure out my own questions.

KATHLEEN: What questions?

SALEENA: At the end, I think about the book. For example, in *Dreams of Victory*, I didn't understand why she kept on dreaming. I wrote my question in my reading journal and looked back through the book for clues and imagined why she would do that. I didn't used to ask myself questions. When I ask questions, I know I'm thinking.

KATHLEEN: Why think?

SALEENA: In grade two, I didn't used to think about the books. If I think about it, I find out what I can use to help my writing. I found that books were the way to find out how to write. For example, after I read about Mowgli in *Tales from the Jungle Book* [(Kipling 1985)], I wrote a story at home about a boy and animals who try to connect.

KATHLEEN: Anything else?

SALEENA: I choose books more carefully.

KATHLEEN: How?

SALEENA: I read at least two pages to see if it's a good beginning. I didn't care what I read before. I didn't know it was important. I just thought you grabbed a book, read it, and put it back on the shelf. I didn't care or think about it.

KATHLEEN: Why do you think you changed?

SALEENA: I think writing changed me. And then I found out there were different kinds of books. I became curious. I didn't know there was a difference between fantasies and fairy tales. I like mysteries and adventures. I didn't care what I read before.

KATHLEEN: [*I looked at her and waited.*]

SALEENA: In my journals, I can tell I'm thinking more about the books.

KATHLEEN: How can you tell?

SALEENA: I'm able to think of more questions. I wish the author were there to ask like in our writing conferences when we can ask, ask, ask and the writer is right there.

KATHLEEN: [*I waited.*]

SALEENA: My entries are better organized.

KATHLEEN: Why is that good?

SALEENA: When I wrote about *Rip-Roaring Russell* [(Hurwitz 1983)], I just wrote what he did. I didn't write about what I thought.

KATHLEEN: What do you plan to do in writing?

SALEENA: I'd like to make a mystery or adventure story. I'd like to learn how to write them. I'll probably learn by reading stories like that.

KATHLEEN: What do you plan to do in reading?

SALEENA: I'd like to finish *Golden Mare* [(Hearst 1975)] and begin *Beautiful Joe* [(Saunders 1934)]. I'm doing a novel study on *Golden Mare* and I'll be doing a novel study on *Beautiful Joe.*

It is apparent from Saleena's own reporting about her progress that she is well aware of the writer and reader she once was and the literate person she is becoming. When Saleena talks about her writing and reading, she sounds so much more adventurous than the Saleena I usually see. Her beliefs about the importance of ideas in reading echoed for me Neil Postman's view that "Idea is a product of literacy," (1979, p. 35). Her interview showed she can use examples from her own writing and reading to illustrate her points. I learned of the importance of thinking and ideas in her learning to be an expressive writer and a reader who interacts with text to create meaning. She let me know that books are the main source for her learning about genres, style, and structure. She shared that she is not afraid to express questions which, for her, do not yet have answers. She sees her involvement with literacy as a journey with a destination that is all the more exciting for its mystery. There will be many unanswered questions for her in the challenging books she chooses. There will be many days of writer's block. But I sense that Saleena is not afraid of the ambiguities that come with the territory of being truly literate.

Farhan's Interview

Farhan is the youngest of three boys in his family. He is the best checkers player in the class. He is small for his age but he is also our best baseball player. He is the only one who can catch even the wildest hits. He never brags. To find out about him, I have learned I need to watch closely and ask questions. He sat on his hands as he leaned forward in the chair waiting for the interview to begin. He smiled shyly at me but kept looking away as he waited for the first question.

KATHLEEN: What have you learned about writing?

FARHAN: I used to do short stories because I didn't have much information in my head.

KATHLEEN: What do you mean?

FARHAN: I didn't know many words. When we began to read novels like *Fishing for Trouble* [(Siamon 1987)], *Help I'm a Prisoner in the Library* [(Clifford 1979)], and *Different Dragons* [(Little 1986)], I didn't know the words but I kept trying. The same words kept appearing in the books. When I got older, I had to use more of my brain and I felt smarter and my stories got better. They had more information. Like my story about the Montreal Canadiens.

KATHLEEN: [*I waited.*]

FARHAN: I used to be scared to bring stories to the group because I knew they would ask questions that I couldn't answer. Now I don't mind coming to the group because I know I have included most of the information already.

KATHLEEN: How did you change?

FARHAN: By reading lots of books. When I went for my scheduled library time, I chose two books every day. Really interesting books. That's how I learned how to write. I wrote better stories by reading better books.

KATHLEEN: What have you learned about reading?

FARHAN: In September, I used to read small books and I could only write a small journal entry about them. Now I can read novels like *Prince Caspian* [(Lewis 1951)] and I have more ideas about them because they have more information.

KATHLEEN: How did this change happen?

FARHAN: I used to read Robert Munsch books but then I tried *Henry Huggins* [(Cleary 1950)] and I enjoyed it. It had some parts I could use. I used the word *unless* in a story and I'm going to use the name *Jason* in my next story. The novels are hard at the beginning but when you get about halfway through, it's easy to read, you like it, and you want to go on. You don't want to stop. I don't even need pictures because there's so much information, I can imagine it myself.

KATHLEEN: What do you plan to do in writing?

FARHAN: I'm going to try new things in stories with big problems. I'd like to try writing novels.

KATHLEEN: Why?

FARHAN: I want to write the best stories I can. Lots of people could read them. When people comment about my stories I know they're my best.

KATHLEEN: What do you plan to do in reading?

FARHAN: I'm going to try to borrow four novels that will keep me going for a long time. I'm going to read faster and understand it.

KATHLEEN: Why do you want to read faster?

FARHAN: So I can get on with it and read more books. I'm going to practice. I'm going to take big books, like novels, and time myself.

KATHLEEN: How will you know you understand?
FARHAN: I have to know who the characters are, what the problem is, and what the situation is.

While Saleena measured her growth by the discovery of ideas in books and her own thinking about those ideas, Farhan measured his growth in newly acquired words and information. His favorite evidence was his story about the Montreal Canadiens, which contained all the statistics anyone would ever need to know about that hockey team. When Farhan began to read *Prince Caspian* at the beginning of May, I knew it was a significant milestone. He was beginning to see that a learner is not merely a "dealer in information" (Smith 1983, p. 119), but an explorer of possibilities. Not only was it the most difficult book he had yet read, but he could hardly contain his excitement when he talked to me or his friends about its latest adventure. I haven't read the story he will write after he has finished *Prince Caspian* because he left for India still reading it. He packed three other C.S. Lewis novels in his suitcase.

I had observed Farhan's progress over several months. To hear Farhan focus my attention on the highlights of his reading and his early difficulties told me more about the specifics of his struggling with language than I would have been able to report without his input. The difference between my own perspective of his growth and Farhan's perspective was like the difference between watching a plant growing in my garden day by day from seedling to full flower and seeing those same changes in time-lapse photography. Farhan was able to explain his day-to-day struggles and triumphs with sharp memories and clear examples. My own report of his achievements would have been accurate but lacking in the life that only a firsthand account can convey.

Saleena's and Farhan's reports of their learning were not exceptional. Every student was able to tell me specific information about what he or she had learned about writing and reading as well as beliefs about how the learning had occurred. The students used examples from their own writing and reading to show me more clearly how they had changed. They spoke with the conviction and confidence nurtured during months of daily conferencing about their writing and reading. The importance of their comments about their increased literacy reminded me of Postman's opinion that "An improvement in one's language abilities is . . . to be observed in changes in one's purpose, perceptions and evaluations" (1979, p. 153).

The students answered my question "What have you learned about writing?" with impressive self-insight. Reshma described her new understanding of story structure: "I've learned that every story must have a problem. A good author will solve it. The story must have a high point, the most important and exciting part of the story." In a less sophisticated way, Hussain explained his own view of the importance of story structure and his awareness of audience: "If you just write something jammed with words with no story, they'll stop reading it." Courtney showed me how she valued feedback when she had finished her own revising: "I take a friend and read my story to her to see how she reacts to it." Shawn illustrated his reliance on the class's opinion: "When the group says it's ready to publish without changing anything, I know I've done a good job." Very few of my students could talk about their learning in writing or reading without mentioning the function of the other. Junaid described how he had learned to write fantasies: "I just started to read books and I began to wonder how I could write like that." Naveed commented simply that "I write more because I read more."

When I asked, "What have you learned about reading?" many of the students reported how they had changed from reading picture books to novels. Junaid explained, "I became bored with picture books because it felt as though the pictures were telling me what the story was about. When I read *The Dog on Barkham Street* [(Stolz 1960)] I could imagine for myself." Junaid is proving he has attained the important stage of relying on internal stimuli (Vygotsky 1978, p. 72). Like Saleena, many described an increased interaction with the books they were reading. Courtney remembered when she read *Strawberry Girl* [(Lenski 1945)]: "It's like having a dream. You can go where the book takes you in your imagination." Some described a turning point in understanding, like Reshma reporting her sudden appreciation of poetry. "I used to think poetry was just lines that rhyme. Now I know poetry writers don't just write from their imagination but they take the ideas right out of their lives. They write about what they've experienced." The students often referred to their reading journals to show how their reading changed. Naveed said, "In September, I wrote short entries but now I can write more because I choose better books." Reshma explained, "I've learned that it's not how long the journal entry is but how good it is. Before, I was just retelling the story instead of explaining what it really meant." These students are discovering the truth of Northrop Frye's comment on the study of literature becoming ". . . not something to fill in our spare time but an organization of human experience." (Frye 1988, p. 122).

When I asked my students "What do you plan to do next in writing and reading?" they outlined challenging agendas for themselves. Many wanted to begin writing novels. Some wanted to write a series of novels with the same characters. Most said they wanted to try writing in a genre they had not yet tried. Their plans gave them a sense of direction and gave me a chance to help them achieve their goals. As Jerome Bruner suggests, "The essence of evaluating is that it permits a general shaping of the materials and methods of instruction in a fashion that meets the needs of the student" (1978, p. 164). My students' goals will not be finished by the end of June. I will need to inform their next year's teacher about their work in progress. When my students arrive at their new class in September, they will find their writing folders there ready for them, and tucked into the front pocket will be their own list of what they told me they wanted to do next.

From the first day of September, my students and I had been building a community of collaborative learners whose strength came from an increasing self-awareness. My students knew that I was passionate about them becoming the best writers and readers they could be. My aim was for them to be able to learn to use their own and each other's strengths to become independent learners. Amanda had struggled with reading during her grade two year. Although she had a cultural background rich in story-telling, she found it difficult to match the achievements of her closest friends. She began grade three feeling frustrated by her slow progress, and she nearly resigned herself to the limits her reading experiences imposed. Her friends and I encouraged her to continue reading. She has just finished *Ramona the Pest* (Cleary 1950). At the end of her interview, she shared her feelings about becoming a better reader and writer: "I thought my ideas were from another planet. I felt like an alien. I'm human now for sure. The ideas are from my own mind. It feels like I'm not a little kid but that I'm writing and reading stories as an adult." My students' self-evaluations proved to me that they have ful-filled my goals for them and, more importantly, they know it for themselves.

References

Bruner, Jerome S. 1978. *Toward a Theory of Instruction*. Cambridge, MA: The Belknap Press.

Donaldson, Margaret. 1978. *Children's Minds*. New York: W.W. Norton and Co.

Frye, Northrop. 1988. *On Education*. Markham: Fitzhenry and Whiteside.

Graves, Donald H. 1990. *Discover Your Own Literacy*. Portsmouth, NH: Heinemann.

Postman, Neil. 1979. *Teaching as a Conserving Activity*. New York: Dell Publishing Co.

Smith, Frank. 1983. *Essays into Literacy*. Portsmouth, NH: Heinemann.

Vygotsky, L.S. 1978. *Mind in Society*. Cambridge: Harvard University Press.

Children's Literature

Cleary, Beverly. 1950. *Henry Huggins*. New York: William Morrow and Co.

———. 1968. *Ramona the Pest*. New York: William Morrow and Co.

Clifford, Eth. 1979. *Help, I'm a Prisoner in the Library*. Boston: Houghton Mifflin.

Conford, Ellen. 1973. *Dreams of Victory*. Toronto, Canada: Little, Brown and Co.

Hearst, Daniel. 1975. *Golden Mare*. New York: Alfred A. Knopf.

Hurwitz, Johanna. 1983. *Rip-Roaring Russell*. New York: William Morrow and Co.

Kipling, Rudyard. 1985. *Tales from the Jungle Book*. New York: Random House.

Lenski, Lois. 1945. *Strawberry Girl*. New York: J.B. Lippincott.

Lewis, C.S. 1951. *Prince Caspian*. London: Collins Publishing Group.

Little, Jean. 1986. *Different Dragons*. New York, NY: Viking Kestrel.

Saunders, Marshall. 1934. *Beautiful Joe*. Toronto, Canada: McClelland and Stewart Limited.

Siamon, Sharon. 1987. *Fishing for Trouble*. Toronto, Canada: James Lorimer and Co.

Stolz, M.S. 1960. *A Dog on Barkham Street*. New York: Harper and Row.

"THIS FISH IS SO STRANGE TO ME": THE USE OF THE SCIENCE JOURNAL

BARBARA BAGGE-RYNERSON
Oyster River Elementary School
Durham, New Hampshire

*A*s twenty-four first and second graders settle down on the rug in our classroom meeting area, I get ready to record their thoughts on chart paper. "Would anyone like to share an observation from their science journal with the class?" I ask.

There is a great shuffling of papers as each child looks for today's journal entry. Several hands fly up in the air. As each child contributes, I record his or her comments on the chart paper.

MARIA: I noticed gray stuff on the top of the chrysalis.

SUSAN: The chrysalis looks yellow.

SHANNON: The gold stuff looks like chocolate.

TOMMY: The chrysalids aren't interesting.

TEACHER: Can you tell us why you describe them this way?

TOMMY[*Giggles*]: I don't know. They just don't do anything. My caterpillar could crawl up a ruler and stuff.

TEACHER: So you found the caterpillar more interesting to study because he was more active?

TOMMY: Yeah.

CATHY: I noticed little blobs of blackish gray fuzz on top of the chrysalids.

We discuss this gray fuzz for a while. Then I ask for "wonderings"—questions students have about their projects.

MARIA: I wonder if the gray stuff is chrysalis or skin.

LAURIE: I wonder how long it will be a chrysalis.

DANNY: I wonder why there are yellow spots on it and I wonder why it is brown.

88

BRYAN: My question is, do the caterpillars shed their skin right before they become chrysalids? 'Cause I think that stuff is shed skin.

TOMMY: I want to know what's happening in there.

This discussion took place in the middle of a study of the life cycle of the painted lady butterfly. I gave each child a painted lady caterpillar to study, and followed our usual daily science workshop format. We usually begin each period or workshop session by gathering together as a community of scientists to set the tone for the day's investigation. During this time I may give the class special instructions on the use of equipment. For example, during a study of pond life, I had to show the class how to use a siphon to get living organisms out of the buckets of pond muck that we had collected. I may also use this time to give the children instructions about something in particular that I'd like them to attend to while observing or experimenting. For example, I asked the children to look to see if each of their chrysalids had the grayish black fuzzy stuff on the top. I also asked them to think about what that stuff might be. Sometimes I use this time to read a book related to our study. At other times I may need to explain how a particular recording sheet should be completed during the observing or experimenting part of our science period.

Following our initial meeting time, the students go off to do hands-on investigation at tables around the classroom. For each unit of study, the children are given individual journals to record their observations using both pictures and words. During this time I will move from table to table to confer with these young scientists. This is not a time for me to interrogate the children or to correct any misconceptions or false conclusions that they may have drawn. Instead, I ask the children what they are thinking about or wondering. I ask them about how they might have come to their conclusions or how they might find the answers to their questions. I don't withold information that a child really wants. But I do listen carefully to the child's comments in order to determine whether they are asking me for information or they are still looking for their own solutions. I encourage children to discuss their observations with each other and to collaborate when designing investigations of mutual interest.

We end each hands-on session with some time to share our observations and learnings. As you saw in the dialogue which I shared at the beginning of this article, this is a time when the children benefit from hearing about both the information that their peers have gained and the questions or confusions that their peers still have. This time helps us to direct our future investigations and to summarize our new understandings.

My students keep journals both as a record of their observations and as a way of thinking about what they have observed. How then might I use their journals as a way of learning about them both as scientists and writers? In this article, I will take a closer look at my students' journal writing by presenting examples of their journal entries in an effort to answer the following questions:

- How do children change and grow as both scientists and journal writers?
- How does one go about looking at the journal entries of young children? What insights about the child as both scientist and language-user can be gained through the journals?
- How can a teacher help a child develop and grow as both a scientist and as a journal writer?

Beginnings

When working with young children and also with children who are new to the idea of journal writing, I am often struck by their need to create a story. Andrew's writing is a good example of this type of journal entry. Andrew was studying seeds and plants in the spring of his kindergarten year. Andrew had planted a bean plant. His plant had just begun to sprout when he made this entry in his journal (figure 1): "The man is putting water on the flower."

His desire to create a story about the object being observed seems quite natural when you think about the types of writing that young children have been exposed to both in school and at home. The young scientist is relatively unfamiliar with the more factual style used by scientists. So he or she will instead create a story about the object under investigation which is full of action. I've seen young children turn mealworms into Ninja Turtles and bean plants into giant bean stalks for Jack to climb.

When studying live organisms, particulary animals, it is also quite common for young children to develop an emotional attachment to the organism. This often results in the child giving a name to the organism. Kate's first journal entry during our butterfly study consisted of a detailed drawing of her butterfly. Under the drawing she wrote: "Her name is Sparkles."

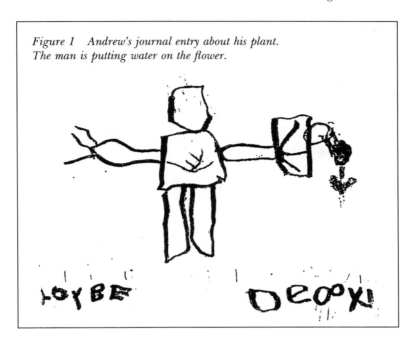

*Figure 1   Andrew's journal entry about his plant.
The man is putting water on the flower.*

It is also quite common to find that a child has attributed human traits or emotions to a live organism's behavior. Mike's observation of a tree hermit crab (figure 2) is an example of a young child's attempt to explain another organism's behavior: "He's prickly. He is a very good climber. He's active. He has stringy eyeballs. When he's sad, he goes in his shell. He loves Stephanie."

When asked about his journal entry, Mike explained that "Everytime we put him [the hermit crab] in the box, he climbs over to Stephanie's part of the table and then he climbs out." I asked him why he had described the crab as being "sad" when he goes into his shell. Mike replied, "When Stephanie goes away, he goes into his shell."

In analyzing Mike's thinking one might decide that he has a long way to go before he will be able to engage in scientific inquiry. But upon closer examination of this journal entry and his verbal explanation of his thinking, I am impressed by the fact that Mike has begun to notice a pattern in the hermit crab's behavior and that he has attempted to explain this pattern. I am also struck by the wonderful language that he uses to describe the physical features of the hermit crab. Phrases such as "He's

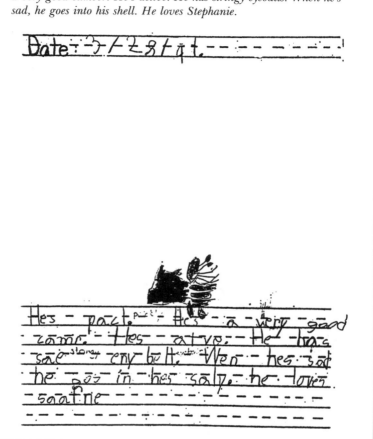

Figure 2   *Mike's observations of a tree hermit crab. He's prickly. He is a very good climber. He's active. He has stringy eyeballs. When he's sad, he goes into his shell. He loves Stephanie.*

prickly" and "He has stringy eyeballs" capture vividly the physical characteristics of this creature.

As children are exposed to scientific writing through modeling and exposure to informational books in the classroom library, their journal writing begins to take on a more factual tone. A full year later, Andrew, now in first grade, has created a scientifically accurate drawing of a mass of frog's eggs (figure 3). Under it he has written observations about how the eggs both looked and felt: "The eggs feel like jelly and they have microscopic eyes and they eat algae. They wiggle a lot."

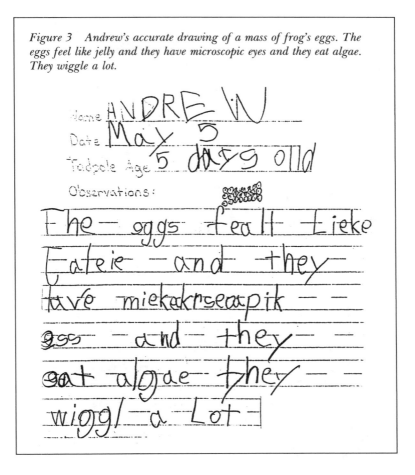

Figure 3   Andrew's accurate drawing of a mass of frog's eggs. The eggs feel like jelly and they have microscopic eyes and they eat algae. They wiggle a lot.

I find that as children begin to move to a more scientific form of journal writing, they often begin by listing their observations. Hoon Seok, a non-English-speaking Korean boy, produced the following entry (figure 4) during a study of life in the aquarium: "They move this way and that way. They move their tails too much. They shake their bodies. Fish color: Purple, white, red Snails are brown and white."

His entry was written independently in Korean and was translated by his Lau tutor. Several weeks later, Hoon Seok produced the entry found in figure 5. In this entry Hoon Seok has moved beyond listing his observations. Instead, he describes a physical characteristic of the fish, the relative size of the male and female, and compares this characteristic to humans: "This fish is so

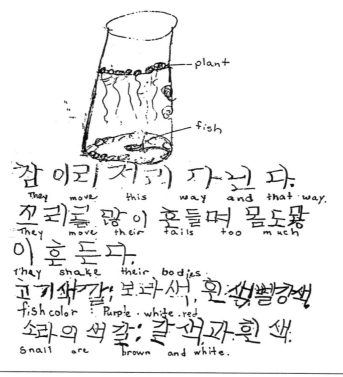

Figure 4   Hoon's journal entry. They move this way and that way. They move their tails too much. They shake their bodies. Fish color: purple, white, red. Snails are brown and white.

strange to me because our people's man is almost bigger than woman. But this fish's females are bigger than males."

Talya and Dara had kept science journals throughout their year in first grade. In this entry, written towards the end of her first-grade year, Talya (figure 6) has described behaviors that require very close observation to be seen: "They have microscopic eyes. You can tap your finger on the side of the tank and they will swim around very fast. They wiggle their tails very fast and suck on the side."

In addition to the scientific tone of her observation, Talya has made note of the way in which the tadpoles react to her actions.

During the same observation session, Dara had also begun to make note of certain conditions which will cause changes in

Figure 5   Another of Hoon's journal entries. This fish is so strange to me because our people's man is almost bigger than woman. But this fish's females are bigger than males.

the tadpoles' behavior. In her journal she made the following observations: "The tadpoles live in water. They eat algae. They are brownish-black. When you blow on them, they will move. We will have to let them go when they get older because they might jump out and we will lose them. If you stick your finger in, they will swim faster."

In addition to describing the different ways that she has gotten the tadpoles to move, Dara is thinking about the ways in which the tadpoles will change as they develop. She has predicted that caring for them when they are older may be difficult.

Gaining Insights about Young Scientists

As children become more experienced journal writers, they begin to ask questions and try to explain what they observe. When

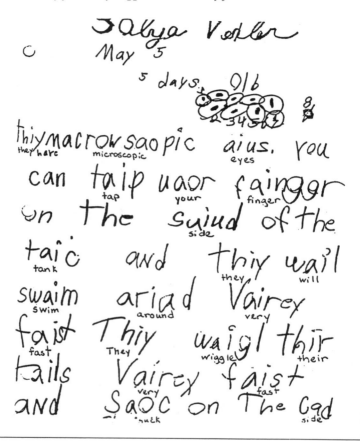

Figure 6   Tayla's science journal entry. They have microscopic eyes. You can tap your finger on the side of the tank and they will swim around very fast. They wiggle their tails very fast and suck on the side.

looking at a young child's journal, it is easy to become over-whelmed by what the child does not know about either the topic under investigation or about written language conventions. When looking at my students' science journals, I look past their grammatical errors, invented spellings, and lack of punctuation. These entries are considered scientific tools. They are a way for the student to process his or her learning. They serve as a record of what the student has learned and can thus be used for further reflection. I do not require that the journal be edited or that it be neat. If the child can make sense of his or her journal at a later date, it is neat enough to serve its function.

During a study of flight, Manuel, a second grader, made the following entry in his journal:

> Pat took a rock and a feather. Pat let the rock go. The gravity pulled the rock down very fast. But when Pat let the feather go, the feather went round and round. The gravity pulled down the feather much slower than the rock.

I'm impressed with his accurate description of what happened when his partner, Pat, dropped the feather and the rock. I am also impressed by the fact that he has attempted to explain what he has observed. Manuel probably has a great deal more to learn about the force of gravity on an object. But he does know that gravity plays a role in the phenomena which he has observed.

At the start of a unit on floating and sinking I asked the class to explain in their journals what makes something float or sink. Alissa, a first grader, chose to answer this question by listing specific items that she knows will float or sink and to then explain the characteristics that effect the objects' ability to float or sink: "A bike would sink because it's big and heavy. A rock would sink because of the same thing. A scissor would sink—I guess. A life jacket would float because it's made to float. A canoe floats because it is a boat. A can floats because it is light."

Her response shows me that Alissa believes that an object's ability to float somehow relates to its size and weight. In other words, light things float and heavy things sink. She has also decided that any item which falls under the category of a boat will float. I am impressed by her awareness that an object, such as a life jacket, can be designed or "made" to float. Athough Alissa has a long way to go before she will fully understand the concept of buoyancy, her journal gives me a sense of what she does know and what experiences she might benefit from in the future in order to increase her level of understanding.

When students understand that their journal is a tool for learning rather than a way to demonstrate knowledge of a content area, they begin to take more risks. They are willing not only to demonstrate what they do know, but also what they do not understand or are wondering about. During our pond life study, Andy, a first grader, is comfortable not only with describing our activities and what he has learned, but he is also willing to record his wonderings. During a field trip to a local pond, Andy helped me carry the pond water around in a bucket.

When we got back to school, we searched through the pond muck for living organisms. In his journal Andy asked: "Why do they [insect larvae] like dirty water?"

This "wondering" offers both Andy and myself an opportunity to plan his further learning experiences and demonstrates his willingness to share what he does not yet understand but would like to discover.

Helping Children Develop and Grow

Much of the growth that my students make as both scientists and journal writers can be attributed to the frequent opportunities that I give them to engage in scientific inquiry and to record what they learn. But there are other factors that help them to develop as well.

An important aspect of our science period is the time that I spend conferring with each child. As I mentioned earlier, this is not a time which I spend interrogating or correcting a child. But it is a time for me to get a clearer picture of what a child is thinking. It also offers me an opportunity to ask questions which may encourage the child to take a closer look at something or to look at something in a new way. For example, Damien had been observing the chicks that we had hatched in the classroom. When I sat down to meet with him, he had written down the color of the chicks and seemed to be getting a bit restless. We initially discussed the colors of the chicks and from there the following conversation developed:

TEACHER: You know, Damien, sometimes when scientists are trying to learn a lot about an animal they spend a great deal of time looking not only at its physical appearance but also at its behavior. I'm wondering if you spent a few more minutes observing the chicks really carefully, if you could find out something about their behavior.

DAMIEN: You mean like things they do a lot or things they like?

SCOTT: I know something they like—poop! Look how they eat it!

DAMIEN: Gross!

My suggestion to take a closer look, along with Scott's timely observation, drew Damien's attention back to the chicks and he wrote the following: "The chicks are yellow and orange or brown. Some are both. When they go to the bathroom, they eat it. They are very silly. Light and sounds attract the chicks."

The children also benefit from the time that we spend sharing our observations at the end of each exploration session. In the large group share sessions a child will often make a comment that will spark the other students' curiosity.

The share time also exposes children to the wide variety of responses their peers are making in their journals. The child who is only making comments about the physical characteristics of his or her caterpillar may begin to describe the way in which the caterpillar makes a web after hearing another child describe the way his or her caterpillar lifts the front part of its body off the table. The child who lists only the things which he or she knows about tadpoles may wonder how its tail shrinks after someone else shares a question about how its legs form.

Throughout the school year I watch my first and second graders grow in their ability to observe, question, and manipulate their environment. Throughout their explorations they gain a better understanding of the world and how it relates to themselves. The journals serve as a record for both my students and myself of how that process occurs. In the words of Hoon Seok Chang, "This fish is so strange to me because our people's man is almost bigger than woman. But this fish's females are bigger than males."

RESEARCH AS COLLABORATION AND COTEACHING

ACADEMIC LEARNING AND BONDING: THE THREE-YEAR CLASSROOM

VICKI SWARTZ
Boise-Eliot Elementary
Portland Public Schools
Portland, Oregon

*H*e walked right by me—caught my eye and gave a half-smile—you know, the kind that lasts but a fleeting moment so no one else notices—and stayed just beyond arm's length so I couldn't give him a welcoming hug. It was the first day of fifth grade.

His hair was strangely shaped with oily-looking mousse and his jeans were acid-dyed. Must be the new fad. The neatly pressed thick cotton shirt remained stiff as he walked. I looked down . . . even his socks matched this year! Good grief, he's in yet another period of awkward middle-year's development, I thought. I watched him circulate around the room, chat first with the boys, and then meander slyly over to the girls. I couldn't help but smile. Other students passed my way.

"So what's our read-aloud?"

"Do we get new writing folders this year, or do we have to use our old ugly ones?"

"Do we have any new kids in our class?"

"Will we have writer's workshop in the morning or afternoon this year?"

I suddenly realized everyone was here, sitting around the classroom, chatting with old friends, fiddling with new notebooks and unsharpened pencils. There was a stir of renewed excitement in the air. Perhaps I should get started, I thought—the bell had rung ten minutes ago.

That's when it hit me. We didn't need to get started at all—clearly we were just "carrying on."

For most of us, this was our third year together. Technically, my title had changed from a third-grade, to a fourth-grade, and then to a fifth-grade teacher as I moved along with my students.

We didn't physically change rooms—just grade level labels. I wrote during writer's workshop that same "first" morning:

> It feels *wonderful*. This year there will be no teaching of my discipline procedures, no "establishing" or "proving" of myself as a teacher with my inner-city youngsters. Maybe we'll revise last year's rules and discuss how rules change and evolve, but there is no hurry. Everyone knows the bathroom procedures, where the classroom supplies are kept, and how I operate. Today there is no anxiety about what their new teacher will be like and who will be in their classroom. Most have writing in progress in their writing folders from last spring that they're working on now. I didn't say a thing to start it off—just "It's time for writer's workshop!" They are all on task! I partnered our four new faces with former students and they are looking comfortable. Already Nakiva is interviewing one new girl to make a "Future Topics List" in her shiny new writing folder. These kids just knock my socks off. The few parents who have stopped by haven't had that worried, "first day" look about them. Instead they've just smiled, asked me about my summer travels, and then they've just hung around like they own the place. Yeah . . . the community of learners is already in place! Even *I* had a full night's sleep last night that was void of the "first day jitters" that admittedly affect even the most experienced of us teachers.

Since these entries in my teaching journal, I have followed yet another group of elementary youngsters from the second grade to the fourth, which I will be teaching this next school year. I have tried to recall the painful memories of moving into an inner-city school from a rural, middle-class school five years ago. The first days and weeks were traumatic, and even though I had eight years of teaching experience under my belt, I felt like a newcomer to the profession, ready to throw in the towel. Children talked back, wouldn't listen, ran around the room, talked over my words, interrupted each other, and grew quickly defensive. There was so much angry behavior. Those first few writing activities had less than a 50 percent engagement no matter what I did. How could I intervene? There was too much to be done; too much underpinning was missing. I had *wanted* to teach a more diverse population and broaden my experiences. What had I gotten myself into?

"One year will not be enough," I said to the principal the second week of school.

"That's what I thought," she replied with a knowing glance. With her support, I kept my same students. We hoped that the depth of bonding between me and the classroom as a community would result in an increased sense of safety (remember Maslow's pyramid?) and stability for both the students and their parents (Maslow 1968). We had a notion that the emotional, social, and attitudinal parts of a child—which take a long time to develop, especially for our many "at-risk" students for whom bonding does not happen quickly or easily—are precursors to achieving the child's potential as a person. Perhaps, we wondered, it should be mental health and not academic curriculum that classroom teachers should put on a pedestal. I considered the disadvantages of spending two or three years with a child or a parent I did not like, or who did not like me. I also considered prolonging the child's exposure to my particular curricular weaknesses (I knew I had better beef up my science program!). Although teachers often advance with their students in England and other countries, I wondered if American parents would like the idea.

The results have been startling. The parents, as it turned out, were quite supportive of the idea. Although I suspected and hoped they would be, I still went through an identity crisis of sorts the night before the letters were sent home announcing I'd be the class's teacher for another year. "What if the parents don't like me as much as I think they do?" I panicked. "What if they say they don't want their child in my room again?"

A strong sense of camaraderie developed. I felt it took nearly a full school year to establish the underpinnings that needed to be in place before true interactive learning could happen on a regular basis. The second and third years we have been able to enjoy the benefits. Although we teachers don't like to admit it, it is often Christmastime before we have a handle on what each child knows and needs to learn, who she works well with, how he thinks, etc. It has also become more evident to me that we tend to stop teaching the last few weeks of school. It is easy to say, "Oh well, the fourth-grade teachers review cursive handwriting, anyway," and just stop practicing it with any seriousness. Writer's workshop halts in the early spring so you have time to publish what's already been written. But when I knew that I was going to have my same class I took on a vested interest in continuing their learning. We practiced their handwriting skills up to the very last day of school, and their work was beautiful. Our literature groupings met right up to the end of the year. I asked if any of them wanted to come to a small, informal grouping on plurals/possessives, and added that it was no big deal, we'd be learning about it more in the fourth grade if they wanted to wait until then. Three-quarters of my class came forward.

In a way, I had an extra four or five months each year! By
my second year with a class, I knew where each child was and
could simply carry on in the academic and affective areas. As
students moved to other schools and new students entered, the
new students were literally "taken under their wing" and their
transition was made smoothly and easily. I began to look carefully at what happened in the spring when the students found
out they would be staying with me.

NEIL and JOSHUA: Will we have writer's workshop next year?
["Yes," I answered.] Whoopee! [*As they walk back to their table:*]
Let's write some *LONG* stories together, okay? That will be
good to have writing for two years.

STEPHANIE: Do you like the story me and Tonya wrote? We think
we'll publish it this year but we have the idea to rewrite it next
year and make it twelve or one thousand pages long!

RYAN: I want to read more of those books next year! [*Looking at
sets of literature that we hadn't gotten to this year.*]

JESSICA: What should we do with these writing folders? Use them
for next year? We won't even have to change the names!
Fresh!

By noticing what was happening—and not happening—in my
room, I was becoming aware, for the first time, of the behaviors
teachers and students go through in the spring to prepare each
other for the upcoming "separation." This time of year there is
often a rash of student misbehavior that we often dismiss as
"spring fever" that can be at least partially interpreted as students
beginning to separate from their teacher and their class. Teachers begin "letting go" by describing the next grade level: "You'll
have more homework in the fifth grade," "Next year you'll do
three reports and your lunch will be later," etc.—sometimes even
in an almost threatening way. With lowered teacher interest and
drive to forge ahead with curricula that will need to come to a
grinding halt soon anyway, students begin that separation process. By the last couple of weeks of school, some of my teacher
friends were complaining bitterly that "the kids were off the
wall" and that "they couldn't keep their attention for more than
two seconds." I found myself quietly reflecting on my class, which
was working for two- and three-hour blocks of time on their
independent science reports, holding their own writer's response
groups on the corner rug, going back and forth between the
classroom and the library for resources, completely calm and
nonplussed. I felt almost embarrassed to say anything. If my

hunch is right that learning is dependent upon the quality of the relationships that are formed between the child, parents, peers, and teacher, then why do we toss these relationships away as soon as they are built and start all over again every nine months?

By the end of the second year that I had my students, a funny thing happened. They did quite well on the Portland Achievement Test. As a class, my group's test point gains were in the high category in a school that scores in the low to average range in both reading and math. Although I was proud of our gains, I hoped that our system's need for percentile ranking and black-and-white accountability would not overlook the other more important "gray" areas of growth that I saw with my students that could not be measured on a standardized test.

> After giving an Informal Reading Inventory to James, he said sheepishly, "Ms. Swartz, do you think that I read better?" He was clearly shocked and pleased with his performance, even without me telling him his "score" or "level." He had just passed the fourth grade level test, only missing one question. The fact of the matter was that James had been a beginner reader just two years ago in third grade, and he had gained five years in reading.
>
> "Do you think you can read better?" I replied, to which he smiled, and looking somewhat bewildered, said, "Yeah—I can *read!*"

A few weeks later I asked my principal to come in and privately compliment James on his remarkable academic gains, as I knew James responded to and needed positive statements by people in positions of power. James turned and looked away from her in mock embarrassment.

> "And how did you do it? What was it that made the difference?" she asked.
>
> "I don't know," he said. He really didn't. Maybe I don't either, but suspect that stability, high expectations, and working through a series of behavior problems opened him up, at last, to some learning. James lives with tired grandparents, who believe the difference came through anointment and prayer. Whatever it was, James, with identified learning disabilities and behavior problems, had crossed a very important barrier.

Last fall the Resource Room teacher asked James what he wanted to work on when he visited her room twice weekly. She'd had behavior and attitudinal problems from him, so she had decided to empower him. It worked. After listening to an audio tape of himself reading, he said, "I want to work on reading faster." Bingo! We couldn't have set a better goal for him our-

selves! James worked out a convenient time to meet with her and
went willingly for several weeks until she left on pregnancy leave,
when he would have nothing to do with the substitute teacher.

The issue of "pull-outs" during the school day has long been
a concern of mine. During my first year at my current school
over half of my class received services from the school counseling
program for thirty minutes a week. Two went on Mondays at
9:30, three went on Tuesdays at 10:45, another went on Wednes-
days at 11:05, etc. Many of these same children also qualified for
pull-out programs for help in reading, math, or speech services.
Some hated to leave in the middle of activities. Some watched
the clock to remember their time, which lessened their full
involvement in what we were doing. Some didn't mind leaving
because it got them out of work, and they enjoyed the quick
exception-making that the general confusion spun me into: "Oh,
you weren't here when we did that? Well, I guess you don't need
to do it then." I certainly could not keep track of who was where,
when. How could my whole language activities, that were integrated around our topic of study, ever have continuity for these
kids who were in and out so much?

Although I do not feel as well-trained as the school's Child
Development Specialist (the counselor) or reading specialist, I
have realized that it is me, with whom the children (and their
parents) have bonded and with whom they spend their whole
school day, that will make the most difference. It seemed to me
that the kids who qualified for the most pull-out programs were
the ones least likely to easily make transitions out of and then
back into a busy classroom. As a school we began questioning the
pull-out model, and most of our specialists began experimenting
with in-class support. With rare exceptions, my students no
longer leave the classroom to attend Chapter 1, speech therapy,
language enrichment, or counseling. The results? For us, the
approach is working. My whole classroom revolves around a
focus on mental health and social skills which is overtly smuggled
into all of my teaching. The students have a "home" in our
room that is assured and safe. They are part of all of our whole
language activities and each student meets regularly with me to
discuss his or her chosen readings in a literature group. Their
academic gains have surpassed those gains made in pull-out programs even without specialized training on my part. The difference is that I am their main teacher and their work is all
integrated—not separated—with what we are doing in the classroom.

Today's writing response group was not so unusual—but I looked at it from an outsider's perspective. I meet with five kids daily and each child then calls on the responders, one at a time, to give feedback. First they give compliments and the author underlines "parts that are strong." Then the students ask questions about unclear or missing parts that may lead to revision. "I like your lead, 'It was a dark and stormy night,'" said Chris. Elaine raised her hand and Laura called on her. "How did the monster get on the airplane so quickly?" Once again I realized that most of the compliments and questions I had planned to give had already been given. After two years of modeling and practicing, these kids are skillful writers and responders.

Following the same students has been a marvelous learning opportunity for me. It has caused me to take a much broader perspective on what I do in the classroom. It has helped me to value and focus on the *process* of learning, growth, and behavior improvement, rather than collect a file of activities I could continue to use year after year with the same grade level. I have been able to stay fresh and learn with my children by building and designing new curricula with them. For many children, I have been *the* stability in their lives. At this point, eight teachers on our staff have tried staying with their classes for more than a year, and the response has been positive. All experienced the same pangs of panic of possible rejection by parents the night before the letter was sent home with their students announcing the plan.

The idea of keeping your students for more than a year has not been free of obstacles, however. Now at our school it is not uncommon for parents to ask how many years their kids will stay with each teacher, or to begin lobbying with teachers to continue on with their class. While many teachers have rather enjoyed this, it has caused stress for teachers uncomfortable with the concept. With one exception that I am aware, all changing of grade levels has been accomplished with voluntary staff shuffling, but each spring this has created anxiety for some teachers anticipating switches not only in the grade level they'll end up teaching, but also with whom they will do grade level planning. I look toward the notion of moving to mixed-age groupings as a natural next step in our desire to build relationships and work on climate, where a fixed number of students stay a second (or third) year with a teacher, and a certain number of new students enter each year. I encountered another problem when my class began to "look" different than other classes to parents and my teaching peers. It seemed as though I had fewer kids with "behavioral problems." I didn't have fewer—it was just that I had a year's head start on managing them. The prior parent contacts, behavior plans, and consistency was working. But an occasional teaching peer still had that *perception*. One year a few parents complained to the principal that their children "got the short end of the stick" by *not* staying for more than a year with their teacher. I feared some teachers that were reluctant to try the idea might have felt pressured to do so. A final unanticipated problem came up when by October of the second year it became increasingly difficult to continue closely planning my curriculum with my "team," because my class was devouring the curriculum at an increased pace. I love to work with a team, but realized that while the other classrooms were still spending needed time on management and discipline, I needed to move forward.

There is so much joy and hope in teaching that must be shared. Most teachers leave the profession within the first five years on the job. They cite discipline, low salary, dull curriculum, and lack of teacher empowerment in decisions as reasons for leaving. They find themselves caught in a cycle of meaninglessness, of routine compliance, of trying to fit into this well-established, out-dated institution we call "education." It is little wonder why they leave. After a while one feels like a robot, a scheduler, trying in vain to "cover" unreasonable amounts of curriculum in short periods of time, of taking two unmatched shoes—current curricular expectations and the real live kids in your classroom—and forcing them to fit together. It just doesn't always work.

I have found meaning in my professional life and have found a way to make a difference. My notion is that perhaps one of the biggest variables in the development of reading and writing—of all subjects, actually—is the depth of bonding between students, their peers, their parents, and their teacher. The two-or three-year classroom is only one of many alternative concepts that look at the child and his or her mental health needs first. I wonder if once this more stable system is in place students are essentially freed to pursue other areas of their lives, like academic learning. Perhaps it is time to bring some of the hidden curriculum out of hiding.

Reference

Maslow, A. H. 1968. *Toward a psychology of being.* New York: Van Nostrand Reinhold.

PARTNERSHIP IN PROCESS: STRENGTHENING THE PARENT-LEARNER-SCHOOL TRIANGLE

RAY LEVI
University School
Shaker Heights, Ohio

GAIL WOOD
Prospect School
Oberlin, Ohio

*D*ear Dad,

My favorite book this year I read is. . . . *Karate Kid Part II*. It is a very long book. It might be a little too short for you. In the book there is a ice cake contest. Who ever can brake the ice cake gets a prise. Evrebody prctly brake there hands exept Karate Kid He brakes the ice cake in hafe but . . . Sato says Give me back my monye. . . .

Love, your son Jon

Dear Jon,

Thank you for choosing me as your reading partner this week. I enjoyed your description of the Karate Kid as it reminded me of the movie. Perhaps I will read the book some day, too. Now I would like to tell you about a book that I read as a child. Unfortunately, it was so many years ago, that I am not certain of the exact title or author. It is entitled *The Black Panther at Indianapolis* by Patrick O'Connor. (You may remember that I once borrowed it from the library for you to read, but I don't think that you did.). . . . I remember how much I enjoyed reading about the Black Panther and its driver, and I would hope that you may some day read about them too. Please let me know if you enjoyed it.

Love, Dad

Dear Dad,

I still remember about Black Panther in Indianapolis. It sounds like a nice book. One thing I remember is it's 300 pages long. I might have to wait another year or two to catch up with the story. I think your letter is magnificent. I think I would like the book.

Love, Jon

Jon's exchange with his father demonstrates an enthusiasm for literature as well as pleasure in written communication about material he has read. It might be difficult to realize that he was completing homework. These are hardly the traditional spelling worksheet assignments that most families and teachers associate with evening study. Jon and his father were participants in a program Gail Wood and I designed to encourage involvement of families in their children's literacy development. We hoped that actively involving parents in the reading-writing process would foster understanding and support of process-oriented learning environments that contrasted with their own school experiences. Families would also develop patterns for responding to literature and writing that could carry over into their everyday lives. As an outgrowth of a joint research project, this program reflected an attempt to create a climate in which our students—second graders in a suburban Cleveland independent school, and third- and fourth-grade students in an Ohio public school in a small town—could trust parents as resources for meaningful feedback and know that their efforts were valued by their families. In short, this program represented an effort to strengthen the parent-learner-school triangle.

Home Study: Family Participation in a Process Approach

Gail and I drove the 350 miles of farmland between Bloomington, Indiana and Cleveland four times to attend a teacher-as-researcher course at Indiana University. Thirty-two hours of car travel provided extensive opportunities to address curricular issues in our classrooms. We were even afforded sufficient time to consider a systematic approach to program development for our students. Notes scribbled along the interstate were refined and became the questions that guided our project: Can parents learn to work with their children in the writing process in a positive, helpful manner? Will parents, through this participation, become more confident as observers of their children's development? Will students see this parental involvement as positive and beneficial? Our work was guided by a recognition of the impact that home experiences have on children's oral language development (Wells 1986) and success as readers and writers at school (Taylor 1983). Advocates of parent empowerment in school settings, like Arlene Silberman (1989), encourage family understanding and involvement with writing.

Our practical task was designing an engaging project for children that would also interest families. We decided to use pleasure reading and letter writing as our focus. We asked children to spend some time each evening reading either independently or with members of their families. We invited students to borrow books from classroom shelves, thereby supplementing home and public library collections. We also asked them to write letters responding to some of the material they read. We chose the letter writing format for several reasons: it would foster dialogue about books among the children as well as families; rather than producing homework in a timely fashion to satisfy a requirement, students would have an identified audience awaiting a letter; and finally, we hoped that the purpose of editing would be reinforced as peers and adults responded to the manuscripts.

We asked the children to share their letters with an older family member before bringing the letters to school on Friday. Parents listened to their children's letters and responded using a three-step conference guideline described on family information forms sent home each Monday. This technique, illustrated in figure 1, paralleled classroom practices between teachers and students. We encouraged students to thank parents for feedback and consider revising the letter they had shared and discussed.

To introduce the process, Gail and I wrote letters to parents and spoke at length during Open House parent meetings. We were concerned that lack of conferencing experience could lead to critical responses by parents and an overemphasis on mechanics. Although most of the students in both schools had participated in literature-based, process-oriented approaches, parents still expected more traditional spelling homework. But we realized that the potential benefits of this program merited risk-taking. We had to trust the interest of parents to support literacy development. We also trusted our students to bring home techniques established at school. We were very careful to address our concerns directly. In letters sent home at the outset of the program, we both wrote, "The enjoyment of communicating about books may be lost if the mechanics of writing is stressed.

Figure 1   Family information forms

FAMILY READING
INFORMATION

Name _____ Week of_____

Books I read this week:

Title	**Author**
_____	_____
_____	_____
_____	_____
_____	_____

Your reading partner this week is _____

Conferencing Steps:

   1. Retell: (Tell in your own words what you heard/read.)

   2. Respond: (Highlight what caught your attention or interested you.)

   3. Ask: (Ask for explanation for parts that were unclear or needed   more information.)

Parent Observations:

We do NOT expect letters with all words spelled correctly and every period in place. Please do NOT worry about editing for mechanics at this point." At the parent meetings, writing conference techniques were described. I showed a videotape of four conferences. In two of the conferences, children read excerpts of their stories to me and I focused upon the content of the pieces. I also showed how I asked children to work on simple editing tasks like finding places needing punctuation. For most parents, the videotape provided their first opportunity to observe writing conferences. Many were intrigued by the stories themselves. They were also interested in such simple response strategies as "I wonder how your character is feeling" or "I'm not sure I understand this sentence. Can you tell me more?" They noted that I only asked children to focus on one editing task during a conference. The videotape was available for families to borrow, providing refresher information for interested parents as well as background material for individuals who were unable to attend the Open House.

Weekly information sheets also provided space for parent observations, establishing a format for regular communication about each student's growth as a reader and writer. This feedback provided assessment information for us. When Aaron's mother noted that "He also needs to take more time in proofing his work," I responded, "Taking time with proofing is an acquired skill! Hopefully, the conference questions provide a framework for re-reading and editing." At the beginning of the year, Josh's mother wrote, "We are new to whole language and inventive spelling so when he asked for help we said, 'How do *you* think it would be spelled?'" We both shared responses to questions like this with the family community in a "Parent Notes" section of the weekly information form. One example is shown in figure 2. We were able to focus upon important issues related to a process approach and reinforce or suggest effective strategies.

As the year progressed, we added an editing step. We began by asking students to identify several words that they thought might be misspelled. After conferencing with parents on content, students used strategies identified and practiced in class for finding conventional spelling and then made corrections. Additional areas of mechanics were gradually added until students had a self-editing checklist that included the basics of spelling, punctuation, capitalization, and letter form.

Given the age differences of the students in the two schools, the family reading programs were implemented with slight variations. Second-grade children were asked to write one thoughtful letter each week to another person responding to some of the material read. On most occasions, the children were paired with classmates. At other times, parents, teachers, and older students at school served as reading partners. On Friday mornings, the classroom buzzed as students exchanged letters. The children wrote short notes of reply to their partners, responding to questions and usually generating additional queries.

The third- and fourth-graders were asked to write literature

Figure 2   *"Parent Note" section of weekly form*

FAMILY READING
INFORMATION

Name _____   Week of November 6.
Books I read this week:
    Title   **Author**

_____   _____

_____   _____

_____   _____

_____   _____

Your reading partner this week is _____.

Conferencing Steps:

Our discussions and written self-assessments have indicated that the boys enjoy writing their drafts independently. Many have said they prefer writing in a quiet room away from adults. Ask your son what he prefers.

After your son brings his draft to you, please begin by responding to the content of the letter. Continue to use the retell, respond, ask focus questions from previous weeks.

After content revisions have been made, please think about these editing steps:

    Some frequently misspelled words from last week's letters to look for in your letter and edit:

_____

    Lightly circle *four* words that you think are *not* spelled as they would be in a book. Find the correct spellings from your family. Make the changes in your letter and write the words on the back of this paper.

Parent Observations:

response letters each evening. The letters were written in a spiral-bound reading log. In most instances, the teacher served as the reading partner although variations included writing to classmates and pen pals. Gail hoped that the journal format would foster a year-long dialogue about books between student and teacher and help the children develop the habit of regular reflection about literature. Reading logs were brought to school each Friday. On Monday, logs were returned with a letter of response from the teacher that prompted oral and written dialogue.

Gail and I depended upon families and students to help us improve and refine the home study program. Comments and suggestions made by parents and children, as well as our own observations, led us to modify the program as the year progressed. The interactions between Aaron, a capable second grader, his insightful parents, and me offer a view of the dialogues that characterized the dynamic qualities of this program.

Aaron's Family: Observing Changes Through a Case Study

From Aaron

Dear Bobby,

I Like One Book That You might like.
The Book Is Birds Do The Strangest Things [(Hornblow 1965)]
The Book Is About Birds
Pengin Cant Fly
Kiwis Dont Have Wings
I Hope You Rede it

This was Aaron's first letter, given to Bobby on September 15. On October 6, his parents observed, "We're trying to help Aaron think through his letter more completely—to think about his word choice more carefully before writing his thoughts down on paper and, to explain his ideas more thoroughly with more specific rather than general statements."

By the end of October, Aaron's letters were exceeding a page. He spoke more directly to his reading partner, noting that "You can take It out At the U.S. Liburey" and asking, "Is The Boys Name Spinky? Read The Book And Let me Know." During the week, Aaron had read books by Steig, Viorst, and Seuss. His parents observed,

> We continue to be pleased with Aaron's reading abilities as well as with his varied choice in reading material. In terms of writing skills, we both feel that Aaron's handwriting has improved as has his spelling and punctuation. His two most recent letters, in particular show a beginning maturity of content and comprehension. Aaron must continue to *think* about what he has read and what the content of the book means to him before writing. He also needs to take more time in proofing his work.

This portrait of Aaron reflects attention to the broad spectrum of reading and writing skills. The comments also point to an underlying area of tension: Aaron's desire for less active supervision as he composed his letters. His concern was shared by some

other children. On the family reading information form I wrote,
"Our discussions and written self-assessments have indicated that
the children enjoy writing their drafts independently. Many said
they prefer writing in a quiet room away from adults. Ask about
your child's preference."

At this stage, parents were paired with their children as reading partners. A number of families had noted during parent-
teacher-child conferences that their children were not anxious
to address revision questions. I believed that the children might
be more likely to expand a letter through written dialogue. This
correspondence also allowed parents to model ways of commenting upon books.

Dear mom and dad,

The book im writing about is *Robin Hood*. The chapter I'm writing
about is Robin hood the outlaw. In that chapter Robin and his cousin
go to the Place where they all shoot arrows. Will is Robins cousin and
he doesint shoot. Robin does shoot and Robin wins a munny belt. I
like the book do you? Robin is a good man who steals from the rich
and gives to the poor.

from Aaron

Dear Aaron,

Mom and Dad really enjoyed reading your letter. Dad is especially
glad that you have chosen to write about *Robin Hood*, since this has
always been one of his favorite stories. Dad's favorite chapter is Robin
Hood and Little John because it is hilarious. He thinks that it is funny
when Robin Hood gets dumped in the stream by Little John and,
when Robin Hood later attempts to blow his horn, a stream of water
comes out.

Mom and Dad have a few questions which we thought you could
answer.

1. Did you find the language in the book difficult to understand,
   since some of the words are ones that are no longer commonly
   used?
2. Is it true that Robin Hood was once royalty, and, how did he
   become an outlaw?
3. Why is Robin Hood still a good man even though he breaks the
   law?

We'll look forward to reading your response!

From Mom & Dad

Dear mom and dad

The answer to question one: yes the language is hard for me. The answer to question two is: yes Robin was an earl. He was outlawed by the sheriff. to question three Robin is a good man because Robin stole because the law was bad back than.

from Aaron

Parental comments bring the process behind this exchange to life: "Aaron was very enthusiastic about starting this assignment, and again, worked, more easily, when doing so, on his own. Dave and I enjoyed composing a letter together, too—a more creative way to foster dialogue with Aaron about his assignment."

All of us—parents, teacher, and learner—were developing a deeper understanding of the way in which Aaron approached reading and writing through the carefully observed process of writing response letters at home. In early February, Aaron's mother wrote:

I realized after Aaron began his letter that he had written one, earlier this year, on the same book. I thought it would be okay with you for him to continue for two reasons:

1. He really loves this book.
2. But perhaps, more importantly, I felt the content of this second letter showed greater depth and maturation already (in such a short time!). His sentence structure, too, has progressed noticeably as well.

Aaron decided this week to write a "first draft" of his letter and then to make changes—editing but also expansion of ideas, when preparing his final draft. This was his idea, and we thought a mature one. In this way, it seemed to be a bit easier for Aaron to organize his ideas and write them on paper more fluidly.

In May, both Aaron and his parents observed growth in their responses to our *Year End Review* questionnaires. Aaron noted that his letters had changed during the year because they included "more detail" and "words [were] spelled better." For Aaron, editing was the easiest part of letter writing, and the most difficult phase was "writing because I don't always know what words to use." He indicated that his parents were helpful because "They give ideas" and felt that conferences might be more helpful "by talking about the book first." Such a book discussion might indeed assist Aaron when he considers "what words to use." His parents were also able to describe effective strategies. When answering the question, "What techniques work best for you when responding to your child's writing?" they wrote:

> Our response is twofold:
>
> 1. Our techniques to a degree depend on the "cues" which Aaron gives to us. For certain assignments he quite comfortably preferred to work independently and to review them with us, when near completion.
> 2. For other assignments, however, he preferred one of us to sit with him—both for reassurance as well as for direction. This allowed his thought process to become more developed and enabled Aaron to feel more secure about writing his ideas down on paper.
>
> Yes, *we* feel much more confident about responding to Aaron's writing primarily because we better understand the school's expectations as well as the skills that are appropriate per his developmental level. In addition, just as Aaron's comfort level with the assignments has evolved gradually, so too, has our own!

The Dynamics of Taking the Process Home: An Ongoing Program Assessment

Writing letters proved challenging for some of the emerging writers. Jared's father wrote in October:

> Writing seems much less a chore (though he'd much rather be playing hockey!). The last few weeks have led Jared to the realization that he *can* read and write!!

Observations such as these led me to consider some alternative letter writing approaches. For several weeks, second graders were asked to draw a picture showing a scene from a story and write a caption for the illustration. They conferenced with families about the art pieces. Subsequently, students were given the option of writing a letter or creating a captioned picture. Eddie's mother wrote that she "appreciated the 'drawing' options earlier in the year." This seems like a more graceful approach for introducing the project, particularly for students who are just beginning to feel confident with the written word in the fall of second grade.

Parents also suggested a move to a Friday-to-Friday pattern. Gail and I had wanted the children's weekends to be free of school-related obligations. Some parents indicated that there was often more relaxed family time during the weekend that pro-

vided opportunities for shared reading. Weekend reading would
allow their children to begin writing earlier in the week.

In an effort to describe our students' growth, Gail and I compared observations made in the spring to perspectives shared in
the fall. David wrote, "At the beginning of the year, it took me
eight minutes to write three sentences. Now it takes me three
minutes to write eight sentences." In September, Eddie's mother
reported, "Reading is very hard for Eddie, he is quickly frustrated with books more difficult than the 'Wordbird' series
[(Moncure 1984)]." In May, when Eddie had read both *Mike's
Mystery* (1960) and *Mystery Ranch* (1958) by Margaret Chandler
Warner in one week, she wrote, "It fills me with joy to see Eddie
getting such happiness from reading. The *Boxcar Children Books*
[(Warner 1958, 1960)] are a lethal antidote to videogames and
TV!" Jon, whose fall letter to his father shows hesitancy with
longer texts, read *Ramona Quimby, Age 8* by Beverly Cleary (1981)
in the spring. His mother observed, "This was a very long book
for Jon to read in two days, but he did it. Getting him started is
all that's hard, then he won't put the book down."

As we reviewed the weekly and year-end assessments, we
noted that parents focused on specific indicators of their children's growth; felt comfortable with a developmental, process
approach; and, perhaps most significantly, had confidence in
new techniques for working with their children. Tyhesha's
mother wrote:

> Tiny is beginning to read the more difficult words without help. I
> have been helping her with her spellings. She is a good reader and
> likes to read. Sometimes she reads too fast. We read together, I read
> a page, then she takes over. To tell you the truth, I enjoy it just as
> well. I think this is a good idea for parent and child to come together.
> P.S. I enjoy the books she brings home.

In December, Taja's father observed, "She is starting to read
better and liking it. She is starting to think the story out from
beginning to end. Needs to practice on handwriting. Editing, it's
getting there." Parker's father, when describing his son as a
writer, wrote, "Very imaginative: writes long involved sentences
and paragraphs. Organizing is difficult, starting nearly impossible; once begun, it's comfortable; uses complex vocabulary,
phrases, and ideas." Anton's mother described an approach that
she was using: "This week I tried to get Anton to organize his
thoughts verbally and then write them down." Eddie's mother
wrote that effective techniques included

> Not to try to correct all spelling errors or put too much pressure on him to write more. Just point out one suggestion or one area that is lacking. I know now that it doesn't have to be perfect—and perhaps he will learn better from only one or two suggestions/corrections.

And Jerone's mother observed:

> Its been hard for me not to be overly critical. For example, I want him to be able to edit for sentence structure and clarity when he is still focusing on putting capital letters where they belong. I think I've gradually been more accepting of his work and able to give him the praise and encouragement that he needs.

Children generally reported that conferences were valuable. Jessuh said, "It's a good thing to have a conference with the parents because some kids don't tell their parents what's going on." Karen noted, "It was fun because my mom always wrote letters." Ryan observed that his family helped "by making sure the letters make sense."

Reflections such as these address the initial research questions that framed our program. They suggest a growing understanding of literacy development by children and adults and an emerging recognition of the role that parents can play in this development as their children grow older. The families of our students had come to appreciate the quality of their children's work. They were able to watch growth and development rather than holding an arbitrary standard as their expectation. Parents, immersed in a process approach, had come to understand and actively support instructional practices that contrasted with their own school experiences. The children and their parents had experimented with approaches that allowed for dialogue about literature and writing. We were moved by parental trust. Families representing a wide range of reading, writing, and English-language proficiency skills engaged in written correspondence with their children and us.

As we read the *Year End Review* forms completed by children and families and compared samples of student work, we realized that we had achieved goals with far greater implications than we had hoped. We had created opportunities for collegial discussion. Curricular decisions had been influenced by our shared insights as well as those of our students and their parents. In our classes, all members of the parent-child-teacher triangle had come to see themselves as learners. Karen's mother noted, "Gave us our time together, allowed us to express ideas to each other with open and honest feedback." And Aaron's parents observed,

"It is highly unusual for parents to have the opportunity to be so invested in their children's educational curriculum."

References

Cleary, Beverly. 1981. *Ramona Quimby, Age 8*. New York: Dell Publishing Co.

Hiller, B.B. and Robert M. Kaman. 1986. *Karate Kid II*. New York: Scholastic.

Hornblow, Leonora & Arthur. 1965. *Birds Do the Strangest Things*. New York: Random House.

Moncure, Jane Belk. 1984. *Word Bird Makes Words with Dog*. Elgin, IL: Child's World.

O'Connor, Patrick. 1962. *Black Tiger at Indianapolis*. New York: Washburn.

Peet, Bill. 1978. *Eli*. Boston: Houghton Mifflin.

Silberman, Arlene. 1989. *Growing Up Writing: Teaching Our Children to Write, Think, and Learn*. New York: Times Books.

Taylor, Denny. 1983. *Family Literacy: Young Children Learning to Read and Write*. Portsmouth, NH: Heinemann.

Warner, Margaret Chandler. 1960. *Mike's Mystery*. Chicago: Albert Whitman.

———. 1958. *Mystery Ranch*. Chicago: Albert Whitman.

Wells, Gordon. 1986. *The Meaning Makers: Children Learning Language and Using Language to Learn*. Portsmouth, NH: Heinemann.

CHILDREN HELPING CHILDREN: A CROSS-GRADE READING AND WRITING PROGRAM FOR CHAPTER 1 STUDENTS

SUSAN HAERTEL
Cedar Hills Elementary School
Oak Creek, Wisconsin

"We have lot's of fun. We lern alot to. He deosn't understand sometimes but I help him. He can even read a little bit. He likes writing sentinces. I don't sometimes.

"He like's to read to me to. He doesn't realy read he says Wat's going on. I read to him to. he likes wen I read better.

"He lerns so much from Clifford books. Even I like reading him Clifford. He like Curios Gorge I like popouts so deose he. Are favrite is the King Who rainded."

Damion's comments describe his work with a kindergarten student he'd been reading to for the past seven months. They were both Chapter 1 students involved in a cross-grade tutoring program. Damion, a fifth grader, began reading more than ever before. His reading and writing improved, not to mention his self-confidence and his interest in school. The younger child heard many stories and began developing reading concepts important to beginning readers. He was proud to have a "big kid" for a friend and enjoyed his weekly reading and writing sessions.

Cross-grade tutoring provides children the opportunity to read and write for a purpose, to take responsibility, to be a leader, to work with others, and to have success. It has been so successful with fifth-and sixth-grade students in Oak Creek, Wisconsin that it continues to be a major factor in the Chapter 1 program. In this chapter I will describe the growth of the program and provide suggestions for beginning a cross-grade tutoring project.

Program Beginnings

A few years ago I heard Dr. Shirley Brice Heath speak about a cross-grade tutoring project developed in California for children of Mexican origin. These children did not do well in American schools because of their competitive nature. The fifth-grade girls were used to playing a responsible role of care-giver in their families where cooperation and the group were stressed over the individual. The cross-grade tutoring program provided these girls with an opportunity to read and write with first-grade children of Mexican origin. After careful training and practice, the girls met with the first graders. The reading and writing activities lasted all year, and the gains in both academic achievement and the affective areas of self-confidence and self-esteem were impressive.

Although the children in our Chapter 1 reading program were not of Mexican origin, the Oak Creek school system was not working for our students, either. They all had different skills and needs, but the one constant in the group was a dislike of reading. They felt like failures, and they didn't invest themselves in schoolwork.

Training Children to Be Tutors

When the fifth-and sixth-grade Chapter 1 students came to class in September, I explained about the new program, and stressed their responsibility as "teachers." The first six weeks of school were spent learning how to be a tutor.

I modeled how to read a book to a child. We discussed strategies to use before, during, and after reading to help the children understand the story and to keep their interest. We discussed questioning techniques to serve as invitations to bring the children into the story such as: "What do you think this will be about?"; "What will happen next?"; or "What does this remind you of?"

During this time I read several books to them, modeling both good and bad techniques, and posing questions to help them get started. They really enjoyed being read to, and the modeling was a very important aspect of the learning process. Some of the bad techniques I modeled were reading with a boring voice, not letting the child see the pictures, and not allowing the child to make comments.

Of course, I was hoping there would be carry over to all the reading they do. One day Mike said, "All this before, during, and after stuff. We're going to start doing this when we read other books too!"

In the beginning it was like a children's literature class. I showed them storybooks, talked about predictable pattern books, wordless picture books, and concept and alphabet books. As I talked, the tutors took notes.

Every tutor had a journal where they would write their reading plans as well as their field notes about the child they would tutor. The tutors figured out how to take notes. Sometimes we made lists. They needed help to learn how to take and organize notes because some of the fifth and sixth graders did not have the concept of lists going down the page; they made lists all on one line. Sometimes we used graphic organizers or outlines. After we tried several ways to organize notes, we talked about the best way to take notes for each situation.

The tutors read as many children's books as possible. They evaluated each book to see if it would be a good book to use with their child. They made lists of the books with comments about each one. For example, Elizabeth read *A Dark, Dark Tale* by Ruth Brown (1984) and wrote, "Repeat pattern, use this one," or, for *The Very Hungry Caterpillar* by Eric Carle (1969), "It has holes in the pictures, days of the week, fun, counting." Some of them even came in during recess to continue their book reviews. I'm always surprised to see how seriously they take this task, but then their reading and writing were done for "real purposes." For many of the tutors, this was the first time they read some of the classics of children's literature.

They then chose the first book they would read to their child. They wrote down comments for before, during, and after reading that would help their child become involved. They noted good places to stop and talk or to ask for predictions. They role-played reading to a partner. We also read into tape recorders so they could hear how they sounded.

Elizabeth chose to read *The Napping House* by Audrey Wood (1984) to her child on the first day. Here's what she planned to ask her: "Before, I will read the title and ask, 'Do you have a dog? Do you take naps?' During, I will ask, 'Can you point to all the animals?' or 'What's going to happen next?' After, I will show her that at the beginning of the book it was dark, and then it got lighter and lighter, and ask if she liked the book."

As the big day approached, the tutors wrote their predictions about how the first tutoring session might go, commenting on what they thought might happen, and how they felt about the project. Here are some journal entries.

Farrah wrote, "I think that I will get to know her well and tell her that everyone gets shy sometimes. I will talk to her before I go to the story, I will let her talk about the story at the end. I feel good that I come hear and that I get to read to kids and that I learn more and more each day."

Sam wrote, "What I think the first day will be like? I think it will be grate. I will like my child."

Damion, who is quoted at the beginning of this article, wrote, "Read expressive, show the pictures, read fun books, read the title, let them have fun. I think it's fun, but I have a funny felling about this."

The Tutoring Begins

One of the joys of teaching is watching children put into practice and improve on things we have introduced. The tutors didn't disappoint me! On the first day of tutoring, I stayed in the background. The tutors were in charge. Soon they were settled down with their partners, reading and talking. The time flew by! They read several books, I could hear them asking questions, and I enjoyed seeing the smiles and intent looks as tutors and kindergartners worked together.

The day after they read to the children, they wrote in their field notes about their experience. Matt wrote, "It was just great, the kid I had was shy but everything went great. We read Clifford's Job [(Bridwell 1965)] and Clifford's family [(Bridwell 1984)]." Sam wrote, "I had fun yesterday. I like Ronnie. he pays attention. I read a Spot book and he lifted the flaps. Then I took a longer book, he was getting bord so I finished the book and let him pick a book. He took a spot book. I like Ronnie a lot."

One day each week they read to their child. They prepared what they would do, they read together, and then they wrote about their experience. The other days in the week we read and wrote using a reader/writer workshop format. As the year progressed new activities were introduced. For example, the kindergarten children read the large nursery rhyme posters on the wall to their tutor and pointed to the words as they read. Soon how-to-read concept and information books also became part of the program. Again, I modeled reading these books. We talked about the difference between a storybook and an information book. For example, in a book about the concept of opposites, they were encouraged to keep their child involved by letting them name the opposite, give other examples, or point to pictures.

In November, a session was videotaped. As they watched the tape, they took notes and commented on what was going well, and problem-solved any difficult areas. Some of their comments included: "I learned that you can be a little silly. Make sure the kid can see the book. Get the kid involved. Point out the pictures in the book. When you have two kids, sit in the middle. When you do an alphabet book, let the child point to the letters. Let the child hold the book. When the kid reads a book themselves, let the child point to the words."

This group problem solving became an important part of the program and the tutors showed interesting insights. For example, when discipline or interest became an issue—"My child won't sit still. He never pays attention, etc."—someone would say, "What are you doing to keep him interested? Did you ask some questions? Did you let him pick out the book? Do you let him read to you sometimes?" One tutor even asked, "Are you reading in an interesting voice?" The tutors knew that I would be glad to step in and help with behavior problems, but that it was best if they could think of ways to interest their child without me stepping in. There were very few times during the year that something needed to be said to either a tutor or a tutee about behavior.

The Program Grows

The program evolved from there. The tutors read with their children and then began to help them write short sentences or stories about their books. I modeled how to help children hear sounds in words and write down letters to represent those sounds. This helped them become good writing coaches. The tutors were encouraged to help the child say the word slowly. Then they asked, "What sounds do you hear? How would you write that sound? What else do you hear?" If the child only heard one or two sounds, the tutor helped the child write the letters, and then moved on to the next word. They were helping the child discover invented spelling. Here's a sample of one child's writing: "I lk St bks" (I like Spot books).

Sometimes the tutors made books to give to their child. We patterned a book after *Where's Spot?* by Eric Hill (1980). The tutors used their child's name in the title of their books, like *Where's Andy?*, and made flaps for the children to lift up.

They also planned parties at the holidays with games and treats for the whole group. One or two of the tutors read a holiday book to the entire group. I marveled that these tutors, who would not read above a whisper a few months ago, had no trouble reading to the entire group of tutors and children!

At the semester's end, we evaluated the project. The tutors read through their journals to see what they had written, and remarked about how much their child had learned: "She knows more than counting up to 20 and the whole alphabet. Now she can read the little books." Matt wrote, "My kid didn't know half of it, now he almost beats me. I wish they had that when I was little." Becky wrote, "I only got to read one book because my book was 64 pages and the name was *Morris and Borris* [(Wisemann 1974)]. Morris is the moose. Borris is the Baer. Kristina only got to read the title. Oh Ya!! And I asked questions. like, what do you think is going to happen? and What's going to happen next? and Do you think this is going to be funny? And she said 'Yes.' I think so because I tolld her alittle about it before we starded."

The kindergarten children also had comments to make about the program. Every time I walked into the kindergarten room they wanted to know if today was the day for the big group. On other days, I noticed they had a much better sense of stories and basically knew more stories than in other years. They also talked about the program at home. Andy even named his new dog Clifford!

The Entire School Becomes Involved

During a faculty meeting in February, the cross-grade tutoring project was discussed. Soon after that, teachers asked if I would help them teach their entire class to read to younger children. It took three training sessions to get them started. The first session I modeled read-aloud techniques like reading with an interesting voice, letting the child see the pictures or hold the book, and asking for predictions of what might happen next. I also discussed different types of children's books that would be good to use. By the second session, the children had picked out the book they would like to read. Again I modeled reading techniques and they wrote questions for interacting with their child. Then they role-played reading their books with each other. In my third visit we reviewed what to do and talked about what to say when the younger child read to them, and what they would do if the child got stuck on a word or made a mistake. We talked about alternatives to telling them to "sound it out" or to giving them the word. We talked about comments to make about their child's reading and how important their positive comments would be to a younger child.

Usually the whole class exchanges between the tutors and their tutees took place on Fridays. It wasn't uncommon to hear in the hallway a low rumble coming from a room and then to go in and see thirty pairs of children sitting next to each other on the floor reading and talking.

After a few weeks the principal commented that problems on the playground between older and younger children had diminished a bit. Sometimes they were even playing together. Friendships were developing through this reading project.

Teachers, too, have been pleased with the way their children handled the program. They commented on how the children were able to evaluate what was going on and then problem-solve when difficulties arose.

After awhile, reading was not enough. The fifth and second graders wrote a book together patterned after *The King Who Rained* (Gwynne 1970). Each set of partners made a page or two for the group book. Another group made a mix-and-match book. It was interesting to note that writing became a natural outgrowth of reading. At the end of the year we again evaluated the project. When the tutors were asked if we should try cross-grade tutoring again next year there was a resounding "Yes!"

When I asked the tutors what they had learned from the project, they said that they had become less embarrassed. Matt said, "You get over being shy, you can talk in front of audiences." They said they could read faster and were using these story-reading ideas with their little brothers and sisters or with the children they baby-sat for. They had grown in self-confidence and had become readers and writers.

References

Bridwell, N. 1984. *Clifford's Family*. New York: Scholastic Inc.
———. 1965. *Clifford Gets a Job*. New York: Scholastic Inc.

Brown, R. 1984. *A Dark, Dark Tale.* New York: Dial Books.

Carle, E. 1969. *The Very Hungry Caterpillar.* New York: Philomel.

Gwynne, F. 1970. *The King Who Rained.* New York: Prentice-Hall.

Hill, E. 1980. *Where's Spot?* New York: Putnam.

Rey, H.A. 1941. *Curious George.* Boston, MA: Houghton Mifflin Company.

Wiseman, B. 1974. *Morris and Borris.* New York: Dodd, Mead, & Co.

Wood, A. 1984. *The Napping House.* New York: Harcourt Brace Jovanovich.

RESEARCH
AS ART – ART AS
RESEARCH

Author Interview

JEAN CRAIGHEAD GEORGE

LISA LENZ
Wilson School
West Caldwell, New Jersey

*T*he first year I began to teach, I asked my fourth graders to teach me about children's literature. They began by reintroducing me to the books of Jean Craighead George. When I was their age, I'd loved reading *My Side Of The Mountain* (1959). Its account of an adolescent living on his own in New York's Catskill Mountains made the wilderness come alive for me and affirmed my own growing sense of adventure. I was thrilled to discover her more recent books along with my class. Using Jean Craighead George's books, we set off that first winter on journeys to places as remote as the tundra of Alaska's North Slope and as near to us as the challenges in our own lives.

Last March, I had the chance to meet Jean Craighead George at her home in Chappaqua, New York. We spoke at her dining room table, accompanied by Qimmiq, a huge, friendly malamute whose buzz saw voice kept breaking into our conversation. Jean embodies the spirit of curiosity and adventure that is typical of the characters she creates. As we sipped our tea, she told me about the time she jumped into rapid # 179 of the Colorado River so she would know how to describe the experience accurately in her book *River Rats, Inc.* (1979). The range of her research has never been limited to things that can be recorded in print. On a shelf in the adjoining study stood a number of small, accordian-pleated blank books she'd bought at a Japanese book store in New York. Each was filled with the vivid pen and ink sketches she does as part of her on-site research.

We began our conversation by talking about the influences in her childhood that fostered the blend of passions that has helped to make her books so unique: her interest in the wilderness, her sense of self-reliance, and her love of writing.

JEAN: I grew up in a family of naturalists. My brothers and I spent most of our time out in the woods or raising animals at home. *My Side Of The Mountain* is the story of all the things we actually did as kids: making fish hooks, practicing falconry, living off the land. My father, who was an entomologist and lover of the wilderness, taught us these things.

We were also encouraged to read as children. I remember when I read *Gay-Neck: The Story of a Pigeon*, by Dhan Gopal Mukerji (1927), the seventh Newbery Award Medal book. I was thrilled to read that little boys in Calcutta raised pigeons, which was exactly the sort of thing my brothers and I were doing. It was exciting to learn that children in another country were doing what we were doing, raising animals and learning.

LISA: At what point did you know that you wanted to be a writer?

JEAN: Third grade. I really knew then that I wanted to be a writer. I loved words. You see, I had identical twin brothers who were a team and off together on projects most of the time. I was alone a lot and since writing poetry came easily, I wrote more and more. I had one teacher in the third grade who encouraged me.

LISA: Did she encourage you by letting you write in school?

JEAN: Not quite. Mrs. Clark sent the class to the blackboard to do arithmetic problems but I couldn't do mine. So I wrote a poem, sat down, and waited for the lightning to strike. Mrs. Clark came up to me and said quietly, "Jean, that's a very good poem. Keep writing!" She gave me books of poetry to read.

With her encouragement, I wrote more and more, not in class, but at home. Schools didn't have writing programs then. I kept a diary for years. Later, in high school, I became the editor of the school paper.

LISA: When did you begin to write professionally?

JEAN: The year I graduated from college. I was a reporter in Washington, for the International News Service from 1942 to 1943 and later for the *Washington Post* from 1943 to 1945. After I married, I moved to New York and worked for United Features and a magazine. When World War II was over, John George and I moved to the University of Michigan where we lived in a tent in a forest for four years. John was getting his Ph.D. and studied all the birds around us, banded them, followed them, observed their daily behavior.

I wrote my first book, *Vulpes, The Red Fox* (1948), about a hunter I knew in the Potomac River country. He had told me stories about a red fox and his hound dog. The fox would come to the edge of the woods every night and call to the hound. The hunter would then turn him loose and the fox would lead him merrily over the hills. He loved the chase. I was given a young fox by a hunter and raised her so I would know more about foxes. When I felt confident and I knew enough, I wrote the story of the hunter, hound, and fox.

I took the manuscript to Marguerite Vance of E.P. Dutton. She looked at it and said, "You know so much more about a fox. Go home and write a story from its birth to its death." So I did. That book [*Vulpes, The Red Fox*], to which John also signed his name, was on the Lewis Carroll Bookshelf list.

LISA: Why did you begin writing for children and adolescents instead of for adults?

JEAN: Children love animals. I love animals. *Vulpes, The Red Fox* could have been either a children's story or an adult's. But children found it, read it, and wrote to me. I realized they were my audience.

LISA: When I told the children at my school that I'd have a chance to talk with you, the first thing they all wanted to know was where you got your ideas for your stories. What should I tell them?

JEAN: Tell them that my ideas come from my life. Since I grew up in a family of naturalists, I'm able to draw on the experiences of my childhood. As an adult, I could write from experiences with my children. When Twig, Craig, and Luke were old enough to go backpacking, we would plan trips to the national parks, read about the animals that lived there, and take off. While we were hiking, we'd meet the people who went into the stories.

Other ideas come from reading. I subscribe to a number of scientific journals and I find incredible material in them. I often get to know the scientists themselves and go out in the field with them. I am at present reading a book by Dr. Bernd Heinrich. Heinrich has found that ravens communicate with many notes and throat sounds and work out complicated social problems. They are highly intelligent. Heinrich, of course, is even more remarkable. I have come to know him. He has unlocked the language of the ravens.

LISA: Was there a similar piece of research you were reading when you wrote *The Cry Of The Crow* (1982)?

JEAN: Yes, but I also raised a crow my son named Crowbar, and I got most of my information firsthand from him. Crowbar lived here in this house and yard and would come in and out the windows and doors to play with my children. He thought they were his siblings because he was imprinted on us.

There was a sandbox in the backyard full of the shiny things that crows love. One day, my daughter Twig came into the house where I was writing. "I'm not going to play with that crow any more," she said. "He takes all my toys!" "Well, Twig," I answered, "why don't you slide down the sliding board? Crows can't slide."

So off she went. I looked out the window a few minutes later and saw her zooming down the slide with her brothers. Crowbar was stuck at the top. After a long pause, that bird took off, flew to the sandbox, picked up a coffee can lid and carried it to the top of the slide. Putting it down, he stepped in it and *zoom*—we had a sliding bird. In those days, anthropologists thought that only humans were tool-users.

LISA: It seems that you're first concerned with a topic, an area of interest, and that your stories evolve out of the research you do.

JEAN: That's pretty much the case. I usually start with the environment, then find the characters. If it's possible, I live with the environment and the people. In 1983, when I knew I wanted to write a story about Eskimo whaling—*Water Sky* (1987)—I went up to Barrow, Alaska and lived out on the ice for six weeks. My son Craig is there. He is a biologist studying the bowhead whale. He took me with him on his research out on the ice and among the Eskimos.

LISA: Did his opinions on whale-hunting help shape the character you named Uncle Jack in *Water Sky*?

JEAN: Actually, the attitudes of Uncle Jack were mine. I was really avid about not hunting whales until I got to Barrow and saw how important it is to the Eskimo way of life. It is the cement that holds their culture together. It costs a whaling captain ten to fifteen thousand dollars to get his crew outfitted to hunt whales, but he will take not one cent or sell any part of his catch. He gives it away, a gift to his community.

Whale hunting is quite beautiful. Eskimos apologize to the animal after it is killed. They have much more reverence for their prey than we do.

LISA: That's part of Iñupiat tradition, isn't it, returning the spirit of the animal back to the wild where it can be reborn?

JEAN: Yes. Furthermore, they don't want the animals to be harmed while they are alive. When I was in Barrow in 1978, the Fish and Wildlife Service sent a team of experts to Barrow to explain why they were putting radio collars around the necks of the caribou. The Eskimos from many of the arctic villages came to listen, then said, "We don't like what you're doing. We've looked at the radio collar and it breaks the fur. The fur is their insulation. Don't do it!"

I sat at their meeting, awed to hear them talk about the animals with such great respect. When Eskimos make a kill, they believe that the animal has given itself to them. Whitemen—everyone but an Eskimo is a "whiteman" to the Iñupiats—feel it is their way of rationalizing. I'm always surprised by this reaction to the Eskimos' sensitive appreciation of their relationship to the earth.

LISA: Would you have gone to Alaska to do research for *Julie Of The Wolves* and *Water Sky* if your son hadn't been there?

JEAN: My son was not in Alaska when I did the research on *Julie*. He arrived ten years later. After reading the studies on wolves by Dr. L. David Mech, I learned that the wolves organized themselves much as we do with a leader, a second in command, and sort of cabinet members below them in rank.

I was writing nature articles for the *Reader's Digest* at the time I read Mech. When I told my editor that scientists had found that wolves are friendly, he said, "Go!" I went.

LISA: Was your book, *The Wounded Wolf* (1978), based on some of the research you found on that trip?

JEAN: Yes. That was a true observation told by Gordon Haber, the man who was studying the wolves of Mount McKinley. My son, Luke, and I camped along Sanctuary River and watched the wolves with him. One night Haber told of a wounded wolf he had seen in the winter. A moose had injured him and he limped off to hide. "He's going off to die," Haber thought to himself. Early the next morning, however, he saw the alpha of the pack come up the slope carrying food for the wounded wolf. The leader returned every day until the wolf, who was his beta, could join the pack again.

"That proved to me there *is* altruism among animals," Haber said, then added, "Of course, like all altruism, it was partly selfish. The alpha wolf needed his beta, but it was also an awareness of another individual's needs." Haber's was a lovely story. There are endless numbers of beautiful stories that wildlife researchers see by living in the wilderness and watching.

LISA: Did *Julie Of The Wolves* stem from a true story about someone who was lost out on the tundra, someone who learned to survive with the help of a wolf pack?

JEAN: No, *Julie* is not a true story, but it could be. In the Arctic, if an Eskimo is running out of food, he watches the ravens because they follow wolves and feed on their kill. Eskimos know that if they're really in trouble, they can follow the ravens to a wolf kill. And they do. Their cultural stories contain many legends about people and wolves. In fact, they say that the first Iñupiat people were wolves before the earth turned over—from darkness into the light. Wolves are very friendly animals. Children's literature has done them a disservice with stories about the big, bad wolf.

LISA: And yet the fourth and fifth graders I know never seem to confuse the wolves of fairy tales with the wolf pack in *Julie Of The Wolves*. They feel affectionate towards them, as if they were Julie's adopted family.

Most of your protagonists seem to be very much like Julie, just on the verge of adolescence.

JEAN: I like to write about the thirteen-or fourteen-year-old who is approaching maturity. There are important decisions to be made at this time of life, decisions like Julie's—which choice to make. This age group likes *My Side Of The Mountain*, because they think they're ready to be independent. Parental pressure is preventing them from making their own decisions and they wish to be free and on their own.

LISA: So many books for adolescents deal with the idea of kids trying to find a sense of who they are. In your books, and in those by Gary Paulsen, the main characters face encounters in the wilderness that help them to figure it all out. And so often, animals seem to play major roles as friends and companions.

JEAN: Well, I suppose that has always been part of my own experience. Having animals around me helped me find out who I was. Mankind has a craving to have some connection with animals—farms, zoos, pets, circuses. Animals fill a need for us to contact the wilderness and the earth. Through them, we see ourselves and our role in the scheme of things.

LISA: Is there anything that people seem to misunderstand about writing for young adults?

JEAN: They talk down to them. Kids really want a lot of detail and information.

LISA: Is it hard to weave all that information into the narrative?

JEAN: No, I can't help it. It is my style. I have found you can't give young readers too much information. They're so vitally interested in everything.

LISA: Are you working on a new book now?

JEAN: I just finished another ecological mystery, *The Missing 'Gator of Gumbo-Limbo* (1991). Gumbo-limbo is a species of tree that grows in Florida. The book is about homeless people who live in the woods. They're called "woods people." This particular group lived in a hardwood hammock near my mother's home. In the story a huge alligator who acts as their protector is missing. Where is he? Read the book.

I've also updated *The Thirteen Moons* (1967–1969), a series of nonfiction books about individual animals in their particular environments. The series was first published in the late sixties. HarperCollins is reissuing them with beautiful illustrations by outstanding naturalist artists. And recently, the landscape artist Thomas Locker and I decided we should do a book together. It is entitled *The First Thanksgiving.*

LISA: When you update a book, what do you change?

JEAN: A great deal. Editors should never give an author a chance to update anything. My poor editor looks at the revised manuscripts and wonders where the originals went. But the research on animals has come a long way since I first wrote *The Thirteen Moons,* and I must include the latest research.

LISA: You've written so effectively about the wilderness. Have you ever considered writing another type of survival story about a child in an urban setting, like New York, because the city can be a wilderness in its own right?

JEAN: I wouldn't call it a wilderness. It is mankind's habitat. Furthermore, it was done so beautifully by E. L. Konigsburg— *From the Mixed-Up Files of Mrs. Basil E. Frankweiler* (1967). Although I love the city, I feel so much more comfortable writing about nature. It is my life.

References

George, Jean Craighead. 1982. *The Cry Of The Crow.* New York: Harper & Row, Inc.

———. 1972. *Julie Of The Wolves.* New York: Harper & Row, Inc.

———. 1991. *The Missing 'Gator of Gumbo-Limbo: An Ecological Mystery.* New York: HarperCollins.

————. 1969. *The Moon Of The Alligators.* The Thirteen Moons series. New York: T.Y. Crowell Co. [Reissued 1991. New York: HarperCollins]

————. 1967. *The Moon Of The Bears.* The Thirteen Moons series. New York: T.Y. Crowell Co.

————. 1968. *The Moon Of The Chickarees.* The Thirteen Moons series. New York: T.Y. Crowell Co. [Reissued 1992. New York: HarperCollins]

————. 1969. *The Moon Of The Deer.* The Thirteen Moons series. New York: T.Y. Crowell Co.

————. 1968. *The Moon Of The Fox Pups.* The Thirteen Moons series. New York: T.Y. Crowell Co. [Reissued 1992. New York: HarperCollins]

————. 1969. *The Moon Of The Gray Wolves.* The Thirteen Moons series. New York: T.Y. Crowell Co. [Reissued 1991. New York: HarperCollins]

————. 1969. *The Moon Of The Moles.* The Thirteen Moons series. New York: T.Y. Crowell Co.

————. 1968. *The Moon of the Monarch Butterfly.* The Thirteen Moons series. New York: T.Y. Crowell Co.

————. 1968. *The Moon Of the Mountain Lions.* The Thirteen Moons series. New York: T.Y. Crowell Co. [Reissued 1991. HarperCollins]

————. 1967. *The Moon Of The Owls.* The Thirteen Moons series. New York: T.Y. Crowell Co.

————. 1967. *The Moon Of The Salamanders.* The Thirteen Moons series. New York: T.Y. Crowell Co. [Reissued 1992. New York: HarperCollins]

————. 1968. *The Moon Of The Wild Pigs.* The Thirteen Moons series. New York: T.Y. Crowell Co.

————. 1969. *The Moon Of The Winter Bird.* The Thirteen Moons series. New York: T.Y. Crowell Co.

————. 1959. *My Side Of The Mountain.* New York: E.P. Dutton, Inc.

————. 1979. *River Rats, Inc.* New York: E.P. Dutton, Inc.

————. 1987. *Water Sky.* New York: Harper & Row, Inc.

————. 1971. *Who Really Killed Cock Robin?.* New York: E.P. Dutton, Inc. [Reissued 1991. *Who Really Killed Cock Robin? An Ecological Mystery.* New York: HarperCollins]

————. 1978. *The Wounded Wolf.* New York: Harper & Row, Inc.

George, Jean Craighead and John George. 1948. *Vulpes, The Red Fox.* New York: E.P. Dutton, Inc.

George, Jean Craighead and Thomas Locker. (in press). *The First Thanksgiving.* New York: Philomel.

Konigsburg, E. L. 1967. *From The Mixed-Up Files Of Mrs. Basil E. Frankweiler.* New York: Atheneum.

Mukerji, Dhan Gopal. 1927. *Gay-Neck: The Story of a Pigeon.* New York: E. P. Dutton & Co.

DAFFODILS IN MANHATTAN

KAREN ERNST
The Union Institute
Cincinnatti, Ohio

*I*t was a rainy day in February and I could feel the tension in my shoulders as I worked my way through the sloppy streets, the puddles, and the honking to P.S. 400 in Manhattan where I would observe in classrooms other than my own as part of an internship for my doctoral program. There were new perspectives in my role as a researcher: I would sketch as part of my field notes since drawing brought a more personal meaning to my role. I knew I needed to stay open and playful in my work. I wanted to let metaphors emerge to inform my observations, and I knew my own experience as an eighth-grade language arts teacher would influence my choices, focus, and understandings. All of those perspectives gave me a sense of what to do as I approached P.S. 400, but they did not tell me what I would find. I was beyond the familiar.

The Magnet School, housed in the basement of P.S. 400, is an alternative junior high school on the West Side. I observed the classroom of Stephen Rawl for two months with biweekly visits. My focus was to note how the Lincoln Center Institute program was implemented in the classroom through the partnership of teachers and teaching artists. I observed two dance teaching artists, Mike and Julie, as they prepared the students through movement activities to experience two professional performances at the school.

I walked up the steps of the gray stone building, entered to meet a security guard, signed in, and walked down to The Magnet School. It houses approximately 180 students, grades seven through nine. The nine teachers have enormous autonomy over

143

the curriculum and the structure of the school day. Their philosophy valued experience as a component of learning, and the arts and computers were an important part of that experience. The population is mostly black and Hispanic; parents choose this school for their children as an alternative to the regular public school. Despite the presence of students by some form of choice, there were still the real challenges of teaching and learning. Those challenges seemed especially intense for me, coming from my experience as a teacher in a wealthy Connecticut suburb. I wondered how my experience and my firm belief in the role of the arts in learning would help me in this new research experience.

I took my research tools, drawing and writing; my knowledge as a middle school language arts teacher; and my new viewpoint as a researcher into another culture. As I wrote reflections during the experience and analyzed my field notes, I realized I could not write a linear story. A collage of experiences kept emerging, perhaps from the lack of a scheduled day as I knew it, or the blending of departments, or the constant collaboration of teachers with students. Perhaps the collage was due to what I learned of the life experiences of the students: involved with drugs, living in poor homes—in many cases on welfare, and growing up in broken families. Nonetheless, these students were also immersed in the experience of the school. There was a clear contrast between the dingy rooms and the examples of bright, creative expression blossoming within their walls. Activities initiated by involvement with the Lincoln Center Institute were only some of the many art experiences these students had. Stephen reminded me of a director and the school day a rehearsal, and it all seemed to work. I could not link all of these experiences and images together to explain how one fed into another.

These images led me to tell the collage of what I observed through another collage of words and pictures. As in any research experience, my representation includes who I am, the way in which I understand through drawing and words, and what I was learning as a new researcher. Leonardo da Vinci wrote, "Silence, oh poet, you do not know what you are saying; this picture serves a nobler sense than your work" (Hjerter 1986).

Unlocking the Environment

Shiny red bannisters, all in a line, led me down the battleship gray steps and walls. A heavy red door divided the rest of P.S. 400 from The Magnet School (figure 1).

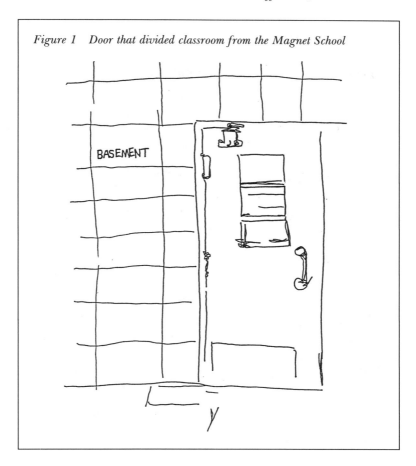

Figure 1   Door that divided classroom from the Magnet School

BASEMENT

I opened the door and was faced with a gray steel door across the hall with "KEEP OUT" boldly and unwelcomingly printed on it. The white porcelain drinking fountain next to the teachers' room seemed like a sculpture (figure 2). My eyes followed a white line down the middle of the hallway. On a tan cinder-block wall hung a huge computer banner identifying "The Magnet School." I was in the right place.

Stephen greeted me, a camera slung over his shoulder, and led me on a tour of "the school": it was comprised of classrooms in just one hallway. Huge drawings—*Medieval Bestiaries*—done by the students were covered in plastic and lined the corridor walls. Another display of drawings of *Gothic Cathedrals in Our Neighborhood* hung on the wall next to the doorless bathrooms.

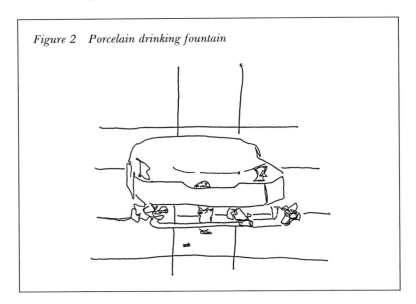

Figure 2   Porcelain drinking fountain

Stephen unlocked his English classroom, next door to the art room, and gave me a preview of one of the settings for his work.

The colors struck me at once: orange walls were coupled with green bulletin boards and half-open mustard tan shades, exposing the cages on the windows. Woodworking benches were piled in the back of the room with yellow chairs stacked on top of them. A dirty wash basin was next to the door, filled with wads of old gum.

He continued to unlock doors: the computer room lined with computers; the art room where students and the teacher were busy making painted panels with images from the literature they had read with Stephen; and the clay sculpture room where bigger-than-life sculptures were created in what looked like an enormous sand box.

The Teacher: The Director of Real-Life Plays

A veteran teacher of over twenty years, Stephen Rawl appeared gruff, but there was a directness and sincerity I noticed as he moved among the kids, whether in the crowded hallways at passing time, talking in the teachers' room, answering a question about the talent show, or settling a fight (figure 3). He engaged with his students through literature, pushed them into encoun-

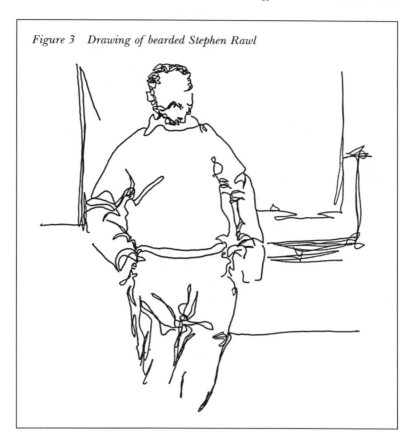

Figure 3   Drawing of bearded Stephen Rawl

ters with the arts, while meeting them with a down-to-earth understanding of their lives.

"The scene is charged with theater," he expounded as he
discussed a text with the students. Passing a student in the hallway, absent from his class the day before, he asked "Where were
you yesterday? Sleeping?"

He took the changes of rooms and schedules in his stride as
he unlocked doors to find his next class. He traveled from room
to room with no stacks of papers or books, no attendance regis-
ter. Instead, he carried his plan, his knowledge of the students,
and his aesthetics all in his mind.

Stephen began his ninth-grade English class by distributing
passes to the Metropolitan Museum of Art. "That museum is

yours to use whenever you feel like it . . . to keep warm, have a cheap date . . . but get serious about art."

He continued by asking a student to read aloud from *A Connecticut Yankee in King Arthur's Court.* He asked the twelve boys in the back of the room and the eight girls in the front to listen for visual images (figure 4).

"This is a good visual," he offered.

Stephen talked with a real interest and directness, while the students slumped in their seats, and one boy ate potato chips in the back row. Stephen explained to me that by ninth grade the more successful students had been selected out to go to alternative high schools, specializing in the arts, mathematics, science, etc. His small classes represented the students left behind. In spite of being left behind he continued to challenge them, show them his sincere passion about the material, to use texts and ideas and engage them to bridge the gap between their own lives and art.

Figure 4   Room of students

The students broke into groups to work on their sketches of the images they had seen while listening to the reading. They would paint them later next door in art.

I drew Stephen as he taught in an eighth-grade class. The sketch reminded me of a Chagall figure (figure 5), full of seriousness and whimsy. He led a drama class of ten girls and one boy in listing topics for their next play: drugs, teen pregnancy, child abuse (figure 6). School gossip was added after he remarked, "Can't you find something funny?" They even discussed rap as a social problem. The class then discussed where their story should take place and the possible cast of characters. Stephen talked slowly, deliberately, as if he was imagining the final production. He censored prostitution from the play, saying parents might object if their child "played a hooker."

The plot and characters unwound as a student took dictation on the board. "Roxanne" emerged as the main character in the

Figure 5   Sketch of a Chagall figure

Figure 6   Listening to topics for student's next play

10 girls
and boy

8 Drama

I want you to make up the play — what happens to kids and what would kids be interested in?

story. Her unpopular status would change as she became in-volved with a boyfriend "on drugs." I noticed that real life was always drawn into the learning. The text of this classroom was the real life of these students and Stephen was helping them think about, look at, and consider real life as the unfamiliar. Whether Stephen was leading the class or watching the teaching artists lead the students, he leaned, disciplined, and moved with them. He took pictures, involved himself, and was always en-gaged (figure 7).

Dance, Decisions, Learning: Say Yes

I got to school late and hurried down the empty hallway. The students were behind the locked doors. A student opened the door to Stephen's classroom. I heard a loud "Say Yes," as Julie, a teaching artist wearing blue sweats, bounced to the rhythm from the tape recorder (figure 8). All of the class—eighth-grade

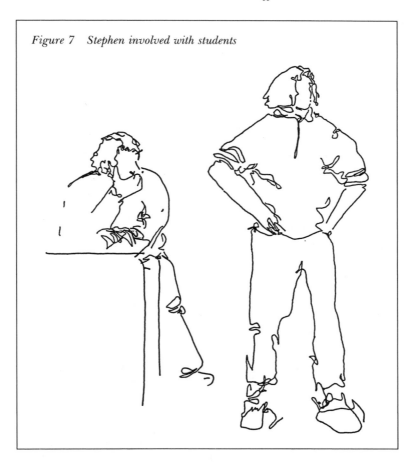

Figure 7   Stephen involved with students

black and Hispanic adolescents and Stephen—were up on their feet bouncing with her, yelling in unison "Yes!" "Yo, now do it without words," she commanded as the bouncing continued in silence.

I slipped into a seat, trying to ignore the wash basin next to me, watching as the students followed her every command: stooping, changing lines, bending, clapping, playing follow-the-leader, and then yelling again "Yes, Yes, Yes."

Julie pulled them out to do duets while others watched. She coached James to move in line with them when he seemed reluctant and was not in unison. (figure 9).

I later learned that she was teaching them a phrase through improvisation which was important to making decisions as a

Figure 8   Julie moving to the rhythm from the tape recorder

dancer. The phrase was from the choreographer Bebe Miller, whose performance they would see later in the month. I pondered how important improvisation was in making decisions as a teacher, in school, in life. These eighth graders, in following Julie's directions, were learning a phrase, a language, a discipline. From my many years of teaching this self-conscious age group, I knew that Julie was involving them through her own risk-taking. I thought about how teaching was directing, coaching, standing next to, and then moving aside.

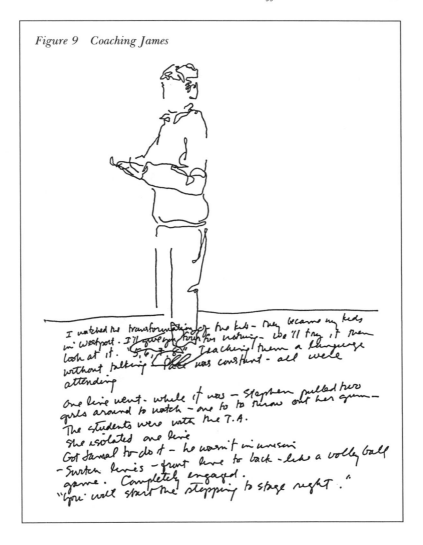

Figure 9   Coaching James

Balloons, Body Parts, Theme, and Variation: Rehearsals of Learning

The students in a seventh-grade class wrote all the sounds they could hear outside the room, then they listed body parts next to numbers on their papers as Mike, a dancer, bellowed out directions (figure 10). Shortly, the students were on their feet making the sounds and using the parts of their bodies while they followed his directions to sit down, turn around, and shrink. Mike an-

Figure 10 Naming body parts

nounced that these would be the first five movements of their dance. First slowly, then quickly, then as if on the moon, they practiced their moves.

In the lunchroom Stephen asked Mike how he thought it had gone. Stephen suggested that next time Mike might want to elicit their feelings about doing the assignment. He offered that he liked the writing but that it could have been more organic.

Wouldn't we all be better teachers if we had constant, helpful feedback on our performance and have the security in knowing it was "only a rehearsal?"

*   *   *

Julie pulled together the entire class of eighth graders to play follow-the-leader as she showed them the multitude of improvisational possibilities (figure 11). They followed her every move.

"Hold your breath," she ordered.

"Hold your breath, you're a balloon, you're a balloon—about to explode! But don't."

"When I start sizzling—let go like a balloon."

Figure 11   *Playing follow-the-leader*

First there was silence, and then the room seemed to swell with energy and these eighth graders sizzled all over the room.

Lisa, a heavy girl, arms raised, watched Julie and seemed to anticipate the next movement, changing with grace (figure 12). Julie demanded the attention of the class through her constant movement and Lisa became her assistant.

Julie divided the class into groups to work on a theme and then a variation; one group was led by a little wiry girl dressed in stripes with the command of a professional choreographer.

Figure 12 Sketch of Lisa

Lisa watches one move and seems to feel what movement will come next.
She moves gracefully —
Wendy demonstrates a phrase
"Kick the kicks small —
"Too hard for me — the recess talking.
Man runs into jiens kids

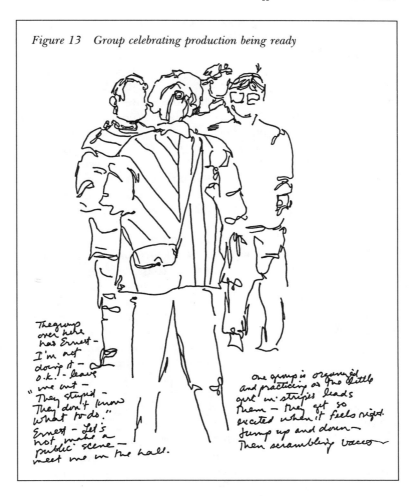

Figure 13 Group celebrating production being ready

The group squealed with delight and jumped up and down when their miniproduction was ready for performing (figure 13).

Daffodils in Manhattan

I left P.S. 400 in April on a sunny day, though traces of snow and winter were still on the ground. I wondered what I had really observed. My journals bulged with drawings and notes from the preceding two months. I had drawn Stephen, the students, the teaching artists, even the hallways. My line seemed to know more than I understood. I found it hard to describe as a researcher this school and my new learning. Was it because it was unlike my own experience, because the organization of the school seemed so organic? Perhaps that was why my wandering line captured my knowledge and my words could not.

As I drove up the ramp to the Henry Hudson Parkway, I looked down into the park. I saw daffodils—brilliant yellow flowers pushing their way up from the snow-spattered ground in a park with homeless persons lying on benches—amidst the backdrop of the concrete, the skyscrapers, the honking, and the people who rushed and seemed to never notice. The daffodils shocked my questioning mood, informed my sensibilities, and brought meaning through a metaphor. The arts were daffodils pushing out, in spite of it all. Eighth graders behind locked doors, moving together, understanding a new language.

As a new researcher I had relied on my own way of under-standing—drawing and words—to capture my observations. I then stepped back from my field notes to begin interpreting the experience, to consider why I had drawn and noted what I did. I grasped that my own drawing and writing fed into each other to help me understand, and that realization helped me know how the arts worked in the same way for the students at The Magnet School. It was not important to try to explain how all of my images connected, or to put the collage in order. I recognized I had been in an unfamiliar situation, population, place, organi-zation, and curriculum. I was able to find what I did know well: kids and school and learning through experience. Through a playfulness in my research I recognized eighth graders as essen-tially the same, whether with a different attire, or a different culture. They had the same self-consciousness, openness, excite-ment, and the need to connect with understanding adults.

Maxine Greene describes the absolute necessity for us to use our imagination to recognize what can be. She writes that aes-thetic experience is a "challenge to many kinds of linear, positive thinking, as well as to the taken-for-grantedness of much of what is taught" (Greene 1978, p. 171).

The experience of drawing as part of taking field notes helped me use my imagination to recognize the collage of experiences in Stephen Rawl's classrooms, and to reach a metaphor that would help me understand the collage. My research at The Mag-net School led me to see anew that learning in school can be challenging, engaging, connected to real life, and informed by the worlds of literature, art, drama, and dance—whatever the culture.

I saw an environment of contrasts, and I learned that creative expression can happen in such environments. Stephen brought the real lives of the students to the classroom and defamiliarized their lives as they created a play based on their understanding. He helped them draw the line from life to learning. He helped them read a text and find personal meaning in literature by visualizing words and then expressing those words through their own interpretations. As I watched self-conscious adolescents bounce to a rhythm in unison or connect sounds to their body parts, I knew they were learning not so much about dance as about themselves and their own possibilities. In spite of the topics they selected for a play, they were still able to use their imaginations to sizzle like balloons, create five movements for a dance, or follow in unison the complicated rhythms of a new language. Dance was one media that showed them the range of possibilities: Lisa let go of her self-consciousness; James shed his reluctance to become part of the group; a little girl found her own way of being a leader.

Stephen, the teaching artists, and other teachers engaged in the process of learning, taking risks with the students, and creating the curriculum in nonlinear ways. They unlocked the doors to learning through their own involvement with many texts: books, writing, dance, visualizing. They learned with the students and the students learned from the models they provided.

I learned that in my next research endeavor I needed to move into the collage, to learn by talking to the students, to be more involved in their thinking, to ask why, what if, what happened, and when, and not just watch their activities. I had hoped that this experience would prepare me for my next research or teaching experience, and I learned that classroom research, too, can be a rehearsal for learning.

The arts and the process of learning at The Magnet School were pushing out, in spite of it all.

References

Greene, M. 1978. *Landscapes of Learning*. New York. Teachers College Press.

Hjerter, K.G. 1986. *Doubly Gifted: The Author as Visual Artist*. New York: Harry N. Abrams.

A Guest Essay

HOW POEMS THINK

DONALD M. MURRAY
University of New Hampshire
Durham, New Hampshire

*W*hen I visit classrooms, I often see a chubby boy with glasses in the back row, paying no attention, staring out the window. I leave the classroom and join him as we become sea gulls riding, so easily, the unseen wind.

Recently, in an essay, I found myself writing:

> I would soon start first grade at the Massachusetts Fields School and it would not go well, perhaps because my imagination made it possible for me to enter the book and become a character, often a character new to the story who traveled his own path through the book, a path the teacher could not see.
>
> When the teacher pointed to a map, my imagination ran up the pointer and into the map, exploring under the canopy of the rain forest, unable to hear the teacher's questions. When we studied the Revolutionary War, I became a boy of Boston, in 1775, three cornered hat and all, a busy printer's apprentice, unavailable for class discussion.
>
> Looking back I wonder how I got through school at all; I attended school but rarely remained in the class. Imagination provided my text. (1991a)

I have always felt sympathy for my teachers and yet I now wonder if it was so terrible that I did not learn their way, but my way. As Elizabeth Bowen said:

> The writer . . . sees what he did not expect to see. . . . Inattentive learner in the schoolroom of life, he keeps some faculty free to hear and wonder. His is the roving eye. By that roving eye is his subject

found. The glance, at first only vaguely caught, goes on to concentrate, deepen; becomes the vision. (1962, 60)

I was learning in my way and I wonder now if there shouldn't have been classes in which all the students were trained in the roving eye and even, perhaps, if the teacher had grown silent, staring out the window, the teacher might have understood the class and the subject better.

Art is, after all, thinking—critical thinking. Life gives us experience but art celebrates it, holds it in place, examines it, gives it meaning.

The academy teaches logical, linear thinking and should. I love to make lists—and Tom Newkirk has shown us the importance of lists (1989)—and in moments of crisis I always create a chart against confusion. I am comforted by the trip from A to B to C; from I to II to III.

Art makes use of linear thinking, but art requires other forms of thinking. It makes possible the trip from B to I to Z and back. Art makes it possible to capture and understand nonlinear life and it thrives on the illogical; the unexpected; the diverse and perverse; the subversive; the as yet unseen; the contradiction; the lie that is truth; the truth that is lie; myth; legend; and the ugly and beautiful.

More importantly, art can deal with the relationship between all the elements in life that logically should not relate, but that interact in our complex world.

Art does all this by artistic thinking. I am going to try and demonstrate artistic thinking, but I must make the kind of apology I discourage in my students and in my writing friends.

This is an early exploration of poetic thought. My maps are scribbles that point out more difficulties than ways around those difficulties.

I write poetry and publish some, but I do not call myself poet. I am aware of the limitations of my talent and my craft, and have never before called it art publicly—or privately. But I can speak with some authority about my own attempts to stare out of the classroom window and make meaning with poetic line.

I use poetry here not just because I consider it the highest literary art but also because it is short and can be examined in its entirety. What I have to say pertains just as much to nonfiction and fiction, which I write, and play and screenplay writing, which I do not write.

Let's start with a list. If you haven't attempted poetry you might play with a list and find you are writing poetry before you know it—a loaf of seven-grain bread, a jug of zinfandel, and thou in the BMW, sunscreened, safe-sex equipped. . . . Well, let's be serious:

Mother Warned Me

Mother warned me not to sit
on cold stone: bone ache,
body bumps, an inability
to produce sons. I didn't
want any. They might suffer
blood poisoning, projectile
vomiting, double lobar
pneumonia that makes parents
stay up waiting for the crisis
to pass, scarlet fever
and the shame of the red
quarantine card nailed
to our door. High fever
shrinks the brain, bad habits
leave palm warts. Mother knew
a boy who choked from eating
too fast; Father knew a man
who yanked one hair from his nose
and died. Stand up straight
or grow lopsided, make a face
and the wind will freeze it.
That's what happened to
Crazed Alec. A Protestant boy
may be tricked into fathering
dozens of babies by an Irish
smile. Beware of skin,
apple, pear, potato, human.
Men who won't meet your eye,
Catholics, especially priests.
Bruises that blossom into
cancer, turned milk, the undertow,
chicken salad put out before
the church picnic, the sin
of constipation. Be regular.
A son who doesn't care for his
Mother, will have children
who never will love him.

Art thinks by putting together what nice people do not put together and it causes us to see our world as we have not seen it before.

Art thrives on a kind of nonthinking thinking, a free-association way of making sense of our world. Years ago some car manufacturers advertised freewheeling—you could disengage the gears and roll on with momentum. That's what I did in writing the next poem.

Every once in a while Tom Newkirk and I sneak out for an early morning breakfast of untreated cholesterol and fat. Pure sin. At one such breakfast we talked of mothers who made sure that we knew things might not work out as we hoped. Very helpful.

Later at my desk, I stared out the window and looked at the strange weather in my woods. Without conscious thought, I allowed a poem to think as I played stenographer:

Winter Morning Out of Season

Winter morning out of season,
mist rises from the land, curls shining
black pines, filters light so there is no

shadow. Lee, our middle daughter died out of season
and I wake from the dream where she tries on
the blue jumper she just ran up on her sewing

machine, twirling, twirling before my eyes and go
downstairs where she has just come home from college,
talking shyly of Paul. I should have been prepared.

Mother warned me that life might not work out
as I planned: my marriage might be like hers;
my store might be lost like father's; Helen,

the favorite sister, died in the Flu Epidemic.
When I was only four, I had gone to the other
side for five nights until the congregation's

prayers hauled me back from Coma. I did not remember
Coma but I was supposed to be grateful at my return.
Afraid of heights, I shinnied up the cliff, toe hold,

finger hold; warned of the undertow I swam; informed
of Hell, I shut my eyes at supper but did not pray.
Still I am unprepared for my familiar woods

made strange by mist filtered light, for trees
that leave no shadow, for April in December,
for a child who leaves before her season.

Our students need to be instructed in such associative thinking, in freewheeling with language, color and line, note and beat.

There is a logic, of course, to that poem, a structure, a meaning discovered, shored up, refined, but the act of thinking made
use of accident. Perhaps we should teach accident in our curriculum.

Another artistic way of thinking is by imagination. Break that
word down: image—ination; see an image and enter into it. Our
recent great war against an enemy not prepared and not willing
to fight in support of a regime that contradicts all we believe in,
combined with my own experience in combat, has made me
sensitive to military images. In Greece I stood before such an
image, a small sword, and went outside to sit on the steps and
began this poem, simply entering into the sword and discovering
its history—and my own.

The Swords Survive

In the museum at Thessaloniki
the guide's voice fades, echoes
from another room. I stand

before a glass case: metal beaten
into armor that did not protect,
tiny swords once warm with blood.

Small men commanded from village,
forced to wear breastplate, plumed
helmet, spent their last night

sleepless on cold stones before
rising with the red sun to attack
other village men who had stranger

gods, served an alien king. I do not
know their cause but remember our
blood cries, how young our legs

felt as we ran toward the enemy.
In this glass case are their remains:
swords bent with use, one dented

shield. This old soldier stands
at attention, in angry tribute
to men like him who were eager

to leave home, willing to believe
in a cause, until the sword missed
bone, drove to another's soft heart.

He feels the ease of giving death
in his own hand, hears his own warrior
cry, witnesses their sudden dark. (1991b)

Art thinks by confronting what it does not want to confront. Donald Barthelme advised "Write about what you're most afraid of" (Gelbspan 1984). I had been doing that in writing about war in poems, newspaper columns, and a novel, and then I remembered good moments in war, was horrified, and decided to confront that horror by celebrating one of those moments that may perhaps be more horrifying than the writings intended to horrify.

My First True War Story

I volunteered to go alone into the winter
woods, find the British moving south
and report back. My rifle at the ready,

I stumbled north through the dark forests
of the Ardennes, leaving deep foot holes
in the snow to follow home. Listen,

I sought the loneliness of war, enjoyed
the excitement of shadows, the sudden
moving branch, the gentle fluttering down

of snow. I hear with skin, feel with ear,
smell to see, my animal self alive to cold,
the Enfield I took from the dying sergeant

so light in my hands. When I high stepped
through the drift at the forest edge
and found myself exposed in the snow meadow

I did not see the German kneeling down,
but heard the firecracker sounds, saw
the snow flowers rising around me as I

knelt toward him, exploded flowers at his feet.
We did not reload, but drew two long tracks
across the snow, smiling as we passed,

then disappeared from each other into woods
where we were once more alone, boy pilgrims
on mission. I remember that joyful day

when I found the British and walked my tracks
back to our lines, a day alone, the beauty
of snow woods and the lonely satisfaction

of the job done. I hope my German found
his way home, sits in a warm room, looking
at snow, seeing my wave as we passed by.   (1991c)

We see narrative as a genre and forget that each genre, each structure and form, is a way of thinking. For years I have been unable to deal with a combat experience. I was digging in under shellfire and dug up a fragment of human bone. I realize that we were fighting over a World War I battlefield, and the experience—then—was not horrifying but strangely comforting. I decided to simply tell the story in a poem.

Bone

My hands digging, digging under the rain from incoming shells—
earth, steel, stone, flesh—found this cup of bone,
this soldier skull. Moist black earth,
blood from my fingers, worms,
a comrade warrior.

This plowed field, where that dumb horse, belly swollen
under those flies that swarm from farmer
to beast, had been a battlefield
in the war before.

I held a hero
in my hands.

The sudden flashes that lit my foxhole revealed
a gap eyed face of bone, a single hole above.
My finger explored its perfect symmetry.

In the dark, as company aid men felt their way
toward cries and moans, I saw the moustache he had grown,
felt his smooth cheeks, stared into his veteran's eye,

shared the smile that had just been taught irony
by war.

He took my fear as my hands smoothed the bone,
until it became the ivory keys his fingers played,
the comb of horn from Tanganyika his mother
gave him to comb her auburn hair before
he left home.

I held his skull to my ear, surprised
by the skirl of highland pipes, beat of drum,
the swords cutting the night air, his feet dancing
above them in silver buckled black slippers, toes so gently
brushing the ground, then his boots marching, metal tabs striking
sparks from Belgium cobblestone.

The shells return and I hold up this cup of bone,
to catch the history of war:
        tendon, muscle, brain,
        shard of steel, shard of stone,
        a boot still marching,
        sparrow wing.

The shells retreat and I pour the cup of history
onto this textbook page the farmer's son will turn
with his bent plow, another horse, when we move on.
My eyes patrol for enemy shadows, but catch
that curved screen within the skull, above the eyes,
where past is held in memory.

A stone house, whitewashed, at the edge of a calm harbor
on the isle of Mull. A door kicked shut and a woman laughing,
turning, breasts now bare, straddles him laughing, tracing
with one finger, the place where a guardman's moustache
will soon grow.

They wake entwined. A compost of sheets. Morning light
reflected from the sea. Curtain blowing in, then falling quiet.
His kilts, my great uncles' Black Watch, adangle on the bedpost,
swaying.

His moustache now fiercely grown, he runs toward me here,
rifle combat ready, safety off, bullet in the breech.
I feel his pounding steps, light reflected from bayonet
hurts my eye. I hear him laughing, see his steel helmet
topped with salad camouflage yet tipped as in the snap
he last sent home, watch him lightly rise as he leaps

barbed wire, then stops right above me here,
hangs in the air,
falls.

I do not feel him as he passes through me, enters earth.

Of course, it is possible to make great narrative leaps in a poem and I certainly did, but it is still story.

Another way art makes sense is by sense—sight, sound, touch, taste, smell. And I am told that when one sense is deprived others try to make up for it. In art we can take one sense or several and explore the world in a primitive way that may turn out to be profound.

One day my wife said as we were riding back from Boston that when she thinks of my parents' home she thinks of brown. At home I thought by color—and touch and smell.

Brown

Left alone in a brown house heavy with the smell of Sunday's lamb
I sneak into the forbidden room still filled with night sounds
and thick light made green by drawn curtains. I never turn on
the lamps with the little orange bulbs, but feel my way into his

closet: rough blue serge, half hidden vests, solemn silk ties,
the belt I know so well, the Sunday morning Deacon's suit,
striped pants, black cutaway. He polished his floorwalker brown
shoes—thwack, snap, thwack—so often they reflect remembered

light. Drunk on father's smell I stagger through shadowed rooms,
dark brown woodwork, beige curtains, brown wallpaper, brown
lampshades, brown sofas, sideboard, library table with black
Bible, redbrown rug, shiny brown floors, return to Mother's

closet, where I stand, proud with sin, surrounded by the silk
of dresses, breathing the woman smell until I hear a key probing
lock and I run inside a book. Mother is again surprised I am not
at play, chose to stay alone in the brown house she hated, flees

to shop, to church, to pace the block as she said she had after
dark when she was swollen with me. Once alone I found, in my
father's locked drawer, left unclosed, the safes that had kept me
from brothers, sisters, left me an only child. Sneaking

open mother's drawer I found an old corset, fragrant with her
woman smell, shaped it on their bed into her. I forced the lock

in her brown trunk, touched the silk of scarlet, pink, silk that
swirled flood rivers of red but was never cut, never sewn.

Art thinks by lying and it is most important that we learn to
lie and to teach our students to lie. It is lies—artistic lies—that
lead us to truth. My mother never had a piece of scarlet silk that
I knew of but those few lines sum up the tragedy of her life
better than anything I've written before. They make me think;
through those lines I understand her better than I ever have,
and in writing them I achieve an unexpected compassion.

I think by lying. I find I am writing a poem about a brother
who fell through the ice and drowned. The word brother never
appears in the poem but Don Graves who knows me about as
well as anyone said, "I didn't know you had a brother." I don't
in life, but I do in that poem—and this one:

The Other Life

My mother imagined an only child,
sold my unnamed twin for folded
cash, never told my father why
his son came home alone. My twin

lived in Iowa and I was sure
he knew the secret of airedales,
how to get oatmeal globs down
his throat, was not afraid

when water rose above his head.
Liked school, could pole vault,
lived in a single family, knew
his parents wanted him.

During my muddy war he braced
his feet against Pacific swells
on a destroyer, later studied art
in New York City, Paris, Florence,

has lived in San Francisco 34 years
with a printer named George. My twin
is lean, bald, but with a beard.
He rides a racing bike, plays bassoon,

high stake poker every other Thursday
night, adopted a walrus at the Aquarium.
Each day he draws fewer lines, watches
as they reveal more, imagines his twin.

Recently, the poet Mekeel McBride gave me an assignment:
write about a tightrope lady from her point of view. Okay. I knew
I could, because the artist thinks by empathy. When Flaubert was
asked who Madame Bovary was, he said, "C'est moi." Artists
have the arrogance to believe they can enter the skin of others,
lead lives that are not their own.

The Promise of the Tightrope Lady

1.

"Step on a crack, break your back,"
but I was the girl who walked the cracks,
placing one foot precisely ahead
of the other, walking myself
to school by squares,
staying on the crack even
when the airedale brushed
past.

2.

They cannot see my pocked face,
my father's nose, my wide apart eyes.
Spotlights glint from my spangled
breasts, glitter off my iridescent hips,
even my high wire slippers wear metal.
They shine as I put one foot down and then
the other,
walking on air.

3.

I hear a voice floating up,
"She never looks down,
that's her secret."
It is not.

I love the landscape of bald heads, shoulders,
of faces looking up, of being high
above the world,
walking a pencil
line drawn
on air.

4.

The tightrope is live, stretched
not quite tight, it trembles to my step.
One night it is U. S. 70, heading west out of Denver
to Grand Junction. Sometimes a single hair
from my lover's comb, sometimes
a snake, sometimes
the back of a whale.

5.

Down there I am all parts:
Mother. Daughter. Lover.
Cook. Sweeper. Wife. Sister.
Neighbor. Mrs. Vera Perkins
not even my name,
his.

Walking on air I am Vada
the Great, held together
by nothingness.
Whole.

6.

He cannot pursue me here. I am not
the good wife in fear of the blow
he has not yet struck, not the one
who listens once more to the story
of his childhood, suffer afterwards
his limp rape.

7.

I am the lady on the tightrope
you came to see
fall,
hoping I will make that one bad step,
the dance on air
falling.

There is no net for Vada.

8.

One night
I will walk
without the wire,
learn to step
gracefully,
gently
out on
air.

Once you can become a tightrope lady, you can become anything.

Those are some of the ways my poems have thought. Other poems think in other ways, and other poets think in other—and better—ways. But our students need to know how stories and plays and paintings and symphonies think; they need to think by art, to accept and understand the world in which they live.

When you see a chubby kid with glasses staring out the classroom window, a skinny girl with eyes that burn through the classroom wall into another world, a boy laughing out loud at the face that has appeared on the workshop page, a girl who puts her book down and continues to read the story in her mind, see if they will give you instruction in the discipline of the roving eye.

Bibliography

Barthelme, Donald and Ross Gelbspan. 1984. "Reporter Confronts the Apocalypse." Boston Sunday Globe, March 25.

Bowen, Elizabeth. 1962. *Seven Winters and Afterthoughts.* New York: Alfred A. Knopf.

Murray, Donald M. 1991a. "All My Roads Lead Backwards." *Over 60. The Boston Globe.* (May 28).

———. 1991b. "The Swords Survive." *The Veteran Poet.* Vol. 1, no. (2).

———. 1991c "My First True War Story." *The Colorado Communicator,* Vol. 15, no. (1) (November).

Newkirk, Thomas, 1989. *More Than Stories—The Range of Children's Writing.* Portsmouth, NH: Heinemann.

Author Interview

BARBARA COONEY

SUSAN STIRES
Center for Teaching and Learning
Edgecomb, Maine

"You will make beautiful pictures." said the
wild waves. Over and over they said the words.
"Oh, yes," breathed Hattie. "Oh, yes, I will."

—Hattie and the Wild Waves

*B*arbara Cooney, a petite blue-eyed woman with a crown of white braids, greeted me at the front door of her Maine village house on an early summer day. She ushered me through the quiet front rooms to a side screened-in porch, where we spent the afternoon talking about her life and her work. An illustrator of over a hundred books and author or adapter of a least a dozen more, Barbara has had a major impact on the world of children's literature. She began her career more than fifty years ago when she illustrated *Ake and His World* (1940), a collection of adult short stories by Sweden's then poet laureate Bertil Malmborg, and an introduction by the American poet, Stephen Vincent Benét. The book was given a full-page review in the *New York Times* in 1940. Her most recently published book, *Roxaboxen* (1991) was written by Alice McLerran and is the story of an imaginary town designed by children at play.

There have been a number of highlights in Barbara's career, particularly her receiving the Caldicott Medal both in 1980 for *Ox-cart Man* by Donald Hall (1979) and previously in 1959 for *Chanticleer and the Fox* (Chaucer 1958), which she adapted from *The Canterbury Tales*. Barbara's three most recently authored books, *Miss Rumphius* (1982), *Island Boy* (1988), and *Hattie and the Wild Waves* (1990), are well-known and loved. *Miss Rumphius* was awarded the American Book Award, and *Island Boy* was a Boston

Globe/Horn Book Honor Book. Barbara feels that although she had written books before, she truly began to write with these last books and is looking forward to another authored book in the future. In the meantime she is illustrating books that she says are about "more than going to the supermarket." The opening of worlds through wonder is central to Barbara's work and thoughts, as she revealed during the interview.

> Last night I was composing a quote for the month of April in a new quotable calendar that the Trumpet [Book Club] people are putting out. I had the picture and the quote came into my head as the dog was jumping on the bed in the middle of the night. The quote is about miracles: the wonder of things up close, the mystery of the far horizon, the magic of clouds, and the miracle of teaching someone to read.

Before settling in on the porch for our talk, Barbara invited me to see her rose garden. Here I was greeted by a medley of flowers of all sizes and varieties clamoring for their places in the sunshine. And then there were the roses, plump and healthy in spite of the Maine winters. Surely, Barbara has a magic touch— a green thumb—for a Maine rose garden is rare indeed. I asked how she managed, and she replied that the roses were mildly protected through the winter and had looked quite dead, but had come back strongly. Barbara laughed merrily and introduced me to her favorite blooms. She knows each one well because she is with them every day. On the porch, Barbara sat on a white wicker chair, shelling peas while I occupied the matching settee opposite her. Flowers have long been one of her passions; clouds are one of her latest passions.

> I drew clouds often before *Hattie*, but I studied the American impressionist painters before illustrating it. Many of the painters, like William Merritt Chase, were living and working on Long Island at time that Hattie is set. I became very interested in how they painted with pastels on white paint and then used a spray. Besides their techniques, I studied how they saw things, like clouds. Another painter I am especially fond of is the Spanish impressionist, Serolla. I love the way he uses sun—and light.

Studying the painters is just one example of the research that Barbara does when writing or illustrating her books.

> I have always done a lot of research. I can't fake it. I have to tell the truth. In order to illustrate *Roxaboxen* I made two trips to Arizona. The first time I went was in early April, but the temperature was

already one hundred degrees. I went back again in March the following year to capture the magic of the desert in spring. There I saw
the *ocotillo* in bloom, and I talked with Alice McLerran's eighty-year-
old aunt, Frances, who played at Roxaboxen as a little girl.

When I wrote the story of Hattie and her relatives—German
immigrants in Brooklyn who became wealthy—I went to the Brooklyn Historical Society. I saw photographs of people and cars, and the
conservatory, in past issues of *Brooklyn Life*. I also read a description
of what was actually my mother's wedding. So the menu in the book
is accurate. While I was there, I visited the Bushwick Avenue house,
which is now a Head Start center, and the hotel. It is the headquarters
for the Jehovah's Witnesses. I looked for the Far Rockaway house,
but I think it is gone. There are other similar houses nearby, but none
in the right location. The Long Island house has been remodeled as
a country club. They took the top story off. I also went to East
Gloucester, Massachusetts where the boat, the *Coronet*, still is at an-
chor. After belonging to my grandfather, it became the flagship of
the New York Yacht Club. Now it is owned by a religious sect. Its
captain, Timothy Murray, is an authority on the *Coronet*. He knows
its history and its owners' histories. He was able to tell me a lot about
my grandfather, including when he came over from Germany.

This quest was personally and professionally satisfying for
Barbara, although it is really not possible to separate these two
strands of her life. When discussing the life decisions that her
characters make, Barbara compared them to her own life.

The life decisions of Miss Rumphius came about because that's what
I did with my own life. I wanted to see the world, and my husband,
who was a busy doctor, said we should wait until the children were
grown. I knew darn well that if I wanted to see the world, I had to
do something about it. I had to step forth. Even though he couldn't
come with me, I would learn the language of the country I was going
to and that was my protection. Then I would travel. I'd take one
child or four children with me, and we would go all over the place.
This morning I had a fax from Morocco, asking me to come to a
festival in the spring. My husband said, "Why do you want to go to
Morocco?" I want to go to Morocco terribly. I can think of a million
reasons why I want to go to Morocco, but first of all is that I have
never been there before.

I didn't want to stay inland all the rest of my life so I bought a
house in Maine. That is a life decision, where you want to be. It
seems like an obvious thing that everyone should be trying to make
the world more beautiful, or better, instead of grouching about it. I
just like to make books. I'm not trying to make them to make the
world more beautiful, but I *do* make gardens. And I love to give
people nice experiences, like a lovely party. And I gave the children

a good time when they were growing up. I suppose that is making the world better.

Like Hattie, I want to *do* something with my life. I was always drawing pictures and writing texts while I was growing up. I wrote about my favorite place, the Maine coast. As a child I thought I owned Maine. I remember resenting it when others said they had visited Maine. I came up here summers to a family compound made up of three houses and nineteen relatives who did everything together. I don't know how we managed. It was just the way we did things. I used the stories of the area and the events that shaped our lives to write my stories.

Barbara went on to describe what kind of characters she portrays in her books. For both Hattie and Miss Rumphius, she looks to herself for the roots of these characters.

All my characters are very independent. They feel good in their own skin, and they go forth. They may be afraid, but they do what they have to do. They are really liberated women, my two, Hattie and Miss Rumphius. I didn't set out thinking about it that way, but they are. I didn't have an ax to grind; it's just that I came from a family with three brothers and a father. They were very, ah—girls didn't make decisions, you know. You were not meant to be in on what was going to happen to the family fortunes or anything. You didn't know anything. Inside myself I didn't feel that I didn't know anything. . . . For instance, my father always wanted to take the boys fishing, and they didn't really want to go. I wanted to go, but my father would say, "Girls don't go fishing." It's sort of like in Hattie, "Girls don't whistle." Girls don't do a lot of things. So I went fishing by myself. And then I had the luck to marry Talbot who came from a family of matriarchs. One was a chemist. The women all were something. Talbot always approved of my leading my own life.

She believes that she began writing well in the last ten years, beginning with *Miss Rumphius* and continuing with *Island Boy* and *Hattie and the Wild Waves*. In all her books she blends fact and fiction, history and imagination, and art and craft to achieve stunning stories. Barbara talked about her need to push past the edges of experience and tell stories that are personally and universally significant. She reflected on her process of writing the three books.

First, you have to have an idea. That you just pray will happen. Part of the idea for *Miss Rumphius* came because there was a woman down in Christmas Cove who threw lupine seeds around. I was wondering for ages how I could make that into a picture book. Finally, I decided to write a fairy story. There would be three things to do, and that would be the third thing. I wrote the story first—because the story comes before the pictures. I wrote it out in long hand and then I typed it. I don't use a word processor although I now have a part-time secretary, and she uses the one I got. I don't dare go near it. I did the same for *Island Boy*, but when I wrote *Hattie*, I typed it out and just made a lot of mistakes. I wrote *Hattie* working at a table in the living room while workmen were turning the attic of this house into a studio.

The first draft of *Miss Rumphius* was written in one day—it is very short—but then it went through six to eight drafts. Originally, it was going to all be set in Maine, but the editor thought that the story should start someplace else. I chose Brooklyn, which is another part of my background. The first draft went quickly because I had the three ideas, and there isn't much else to the story. The end result certainly is different from the first draft. Now *Island Boy*, that was longer and took quite a bit longer to write. In fact, each book gets longer and longer.

I also had part of the idea for *Island Boy* for a long time. I was visiting a friend of mine who lived on an island with a lighthouse, and she had a little boy who was just adorable. I was busy being a photographer at the time and took a lot of pictures. I thought I would make a picture book and that sat in my head for years. When I finally saw the little boy again he was an adolescent with spots! Then I came across a monograph about John Gilley, a man who was born, brought up, and died on Baker's Island in the last century. It was written by Charles Eliot, former president of Harvard, and has been rereleased since the publication of *Island Boy*. I used it as a springboard for *Island Boy*, although I set my book in Muscongus Bay. I eliminated the lighthouse and had it be about a family being brought up on a saltwater farm on an island and how they coped with that.

Much of *Hattie* comes from my mother's life. I needed to recapture things that are vanishing. And I wanted to tell this story as a piece of family history for our present and future generations. Personally, it was a very important one for me to write. I felt an urgency about it.

Since Barbara is an illustrator as well as an author, her writing process is affected by her ability to visualize. She is adamant that the text comes before the illustrations. "The text is like a string in a necklace, and the pictures are the pearls. The drawings come second; the text comes first. Then you wrap yourself around it." There is no stopping the images that come into her mind while she is writing, however.

I knew *Island Boy* was going to be a whole life story. I had a picture in my mind when I began. It was the funeral scene on a beautiful day. I wanted it to end up that way. I didn't have much else, and I didn't know what I was going to do. I did have the Egg Rock, which is one of the White Islands at the mouth of this river. In *Miss Rumphius* the library was in my head, but it turned out differently than I intended. I wanted to have a *brown* dusty old library. For some reason it got too clean. Also, I think I had her house. I definitely had the first house in *Hattie*, and then walking on the beach—sort of an impressionistic painterly look. I see pictures in my head.

I commented to Barbara that I have always been amazed at her ability to tell whole life stories, and even a story of growing up as in *Hattie*, in such slender volumes. She laughed and commented, "Maybe I can do it because I have practically lived a whole life." She laughed again and explained that she had to make Alice Rumphius grow up—and older—quickly. "My solution was to do it one, two, three. It was very easy. It was just what had to be done." Her pragmatic approach is certainly a lesson to those of us who still struggle with those kinds of writing problems. Barbara did not find the aging of Miss Rumphius, or the wedding in *Hattie*, as easy to illustrate, however.

> I aged Alice Rumphius fifteen years with practically every picture. When she got older she was very hard for me. When I look in the mirror at myself, I don't feel that I have changed at all. Then I look at pictures of me when I was twenty, and I can't believe that that fluffy little thing was me. And the wedding. That was difficult. I didn't have that in my head at all. I read the description of the wedding in the paper, and I didn't know how to do it. It was all chrysanthemums and ferns and sounded ugly. So I put it in the conservatory, and that made it turn out all right.

Although Barbara likes her own books—what she calls her "trilogy"—best, she is also fond of many of the books she had illustrated in recent years. *Louhi, Witch of North Farm* (DeGrerez 1986) is a particular favorite. During the interview she talked about some of the others.

> Another favorite of mine is *Spirit Child* by John Bierhorst (1984). It has a wonderful text. It is the Nativity story as the Aztecs saw it. After the ceremonies were banned, they took on Christianity, hook, line, and sinker. Although the Aztecs had a dictionary, it was never translated into Spanish. John Bierhorst stumbled across it covered with dust down at Brown [University]. He translated it directly from Aztec into English. It is a beautiful mishmash of medieval lore, superstition, and love. It is the second known book in the Western Hemisphere.
> Donald Hall's poem "Ox-cart Man" was first published in *The New*

Yorker. Then he enlarged it as the text for a picture book. The story was told to him by an old man up where he lived in New Hampshire. We didn't collaborate on the book. The editor approached me, and we both felt it was right for me to illustrate this one. I'll tell you that winter I was finishing the studio/house down on the water. My son, who built it, said, "You ought to be able to get the inside finished off," and he left for South America. Well, I slept on a little cot, and we had workmen coming in every day, but I did three books that winter!

One of the others that I did that winter was *Emma* by Wendy Kesselmann (1979). It is a true story, changed, of course, but based on a woman named Emma Sturn who fled from Germany during the Holocaust. She went to Normandy, but she was always homesick. When she was seventy-two, her children gave her a painting so she wouldn't mourn for home. She looked at the painting, which didn't look the way her home did, and decided she would become a painter. She painted for the rest of her life and became very famous.

Barbara maintains two studios, one at Hermit Wood, her combination house and studio on the water, and the other in the attic of her village house. She took me on a tour of the latter. It is a large, modernized space with skylights, built-in bookshelves and drawers, windows with a view of the river, and a steep-pitched white ceiling and walls. The furnishings are sparse: a large drawing table and chair, a comfortable-looking antique bed, and another small chair. Only a few tools were lined up on her worktable because her activity is now focused at her summer studio. Barbara talked about her preferences in illustrating materials.

I make the best pictures when I work the way I like to. I get illustration board and I cover it with an acrylic gesso—a titanium white powder mixed in a liquid. I let that dry and that's a whole day. Then I mount really good silk on the board. The gesso has to be squeegeed on to get out all the bubbles. I think, "Oh, my I'll never get out all the bubbles." I work and work until it's all smooth and eventually it dries. Then I turn it over and do the other side because the dry side will be tighter and cause the board to curl. There is no silk on that side, but it must be coated once. I also put it under weights. And I put on two or three layers, sometimes more. Then it has to be sanded down; Talbot is very good at sanding. It is a lot of work, but it is my own dear little system. When I am finished, I have a surface like an eggshell to work on. It is difficult and takes days and days. Sometimes it takes two weeks to prepare all the boards because each picture is a different board. Once in a while I ruin a picture or two, which just kills me.

During the interview Barbara spoke often of other projects past, current, and future. Her energy level appears to be very high, although she claims that she gets pretty tired sometimes. She thinks the Cooney family "is a busy bunch of people" and says that her energetic brothers exhaust her. But she does exhibit a natural drive and energy and derives additional energy from her writing and illustrating. Occasionally, she will have a text to illustrate that she has to make herself work on, but many of them she loves and can't wait to work on each day. This was especially true for her self-authored books. When I commented that she is a hard worker, Barbara quipped, "I used to be a heavy player." But "when I am working on a project, I worked constantly. There are no Sundays. I was almost dead when I finished [*Hattie*]." During the interview she described her daily work habits and workplace.

> I do a lot of thinking in bed early in the morning—or sometimes in the middle of the night. I wake up and I think I'll just solve this one problem and go back to sleep, but it just gets me more awake. Then the dog comes and stares at me, and I close my eyes and think, "I'm not going to let him win this time," but he does. So my routine is to get up and let the dog out. I put a biscuit in his mouth so he won't bark, and then I make coffee. After that I take my bath and braid my hair, and then I get to work. Like that.
>
> When I am working on something I really like, I'll work up until suppertime. It usually gets a little late and I think, "Oh, my gosh, I won't have time to really cook it properly." Then I say, "Do you mind having a TV dinner?" Talbot is very obliging; he actually likes TV dinners. When I finish a project, I will take two days and cook and make bread and do all those good domestic things. Then I'll get to work again, perhaps on a new project or on the inventory of pictures that my daughter Gretel and I have been working on.
>
> Normally, I have to have some sort of privacy when I work. Since the stairs to the attic studio are steep, it is rare that anyone comes up there. But when the workmen were up there and busy, I was busy writing downstairs writing *Hattie*. And the winter I illustrated *Ox-cart Man* and the others, it was easy to work because the workmen were working. It was like a beehive. They would come in early, and we'd all get to work. Then I'd stop and make bread and we'd all have a bread break. They never came and hung over my shoulder or tried to talk with me. They were just busy, or we would yell back and forth. It was a work environment. Really, it was wonderful to work when everyone is working.

Barbara is in the process of completing an inventory of all the pictures that she has left in her summer studio. She has arranged for the illustrations of *Miss Rumphius, Island Boy* and *Hattie and the Wild Waves* to be hung in a permanent exhibition at Bowdoin College in Brunswick, Maine.

At the end of the interview I asked Barbara to sign our school copy of *Hattie and the Wild Waves*. While she was signing it, I looked out over her rose garden and asked if it will be in one of her books someday. She replied that one of the books in which she drew roses, *Snow White and Rose Red* (Grimm and Grimm 1991), was just released in a new format. Still, I wondered about the garden and turned back to claim the book. When I glimpsed Barbara's hands, I noticed that she had a green thumb from shelling peas. Or was it her magic touch?

References

Bierhorst, John. 1984. *Spirit Child.* New York: William Morrow and Co.

Chaucer, Geoffrey. 1958. *Chanticleer and the Fox.* Adapted by Barbara Cooney. New York: Thomas Crowell, Co.

Cooney, Barbara. 1990. *Hattie and the Wild Waves.* New York: Viking Penguin, Inc.

———. 1988. *Island Boy.* New York: Viking Penguin, Inc.

———. 1982. *Miss Rumphius.* New York: Viking Penguin, Inc.

DeGrerez, Toni. 1986. *Louhi, Witch of North Farm.* New York: Viking Penguin, Inc.

Grimm, Jacob and Wilhelm Grimm. 1991. *Snow White and Rose Red.* Adapted by Barbara Cooney. New York: Delacorte Press.

Hall, Donald. 1979. *Ox-cart Man.* New York: The Viking Press.

Kesselmann, Wendy. 1979. *Emma.* New York: Harper and Row.

McLerran, Alice. 1991. *Roxaboxen.* New York: Lothrop, Lee and Shepard Books.

Malmborg, Bertil. 1940. *Ake and His World.* New York: Farrar and Rineholt, Inc.

CALL FOR MANUSCRIPTS

Workshop is an annual about the teaching of writing and reading. Each volume is centered around a theme and features articles by teacher-researchers of grades K–8, reports of first-hand observations that show a teacher in action and include the voices and writing of students and/or colleagues. Contributors are paid. The editor is currently soliciting submissions for the fifth volume.

Workshop 5 will be devoted to the theme The Writing Process Revisited. Nearly a decade has passed since the publication of Donald Graves's *Writing: Teachers and Children at Work*, a book that helped change the landscape of literacy instruction in elementary schools. Practices that were initially revolutionary—allowing for invented spelling, encouraging topic choice, conducting individual conferences—are now common (though hardly the norm in U.S. schools). And even Graves himself has warned of these innovations hardening into orthodoxies or rigid prescriptions for teaching "process writing." To be truly vital these initial ideas and practices must be continually reexamined, transformed, and adapted by teachers. *Workshop 5* will examine and celebrate the evolution of writing process teaching. Manuscripts on a variety of topics are invited, not limited by the following possibilities:

- Are there new "orthodoxies" that restrict our thinking about writing instruction?
- How does talk promote and sustain student writing?

- How can children's writing profitably connect with art and music?
- How can students draw on subjects and resources in the local community?
- How can we assess student progress fairly and usefully? How, for example, can portfolios be used without creating a management burden for teachers?
- How can we respond to student writing in ways that promote growth?
- How does the media culture enhance or interfere with children's writing?
- How can we help students develop the ability to write for a range of purposes—to explain, amuse, persuade, explore, entertain, and so forth?
- As writing teachers, how can we be sensitive to cultural differences? How can we draw on these differences?

The deadline for *Workshop 5: The Writing Process Revisited* is August 1, 1992.

Manuscript Specifications for Workshop

When preparing a manuscript for submission to *Workshop*, please follow these guidelines:

- Contributors must be teachers of grades K–8, and submissions should be written in an active, first-person voice ("I").
- Contributions should reflect new thinking and/or practice, rather than replicate the published works of other teacher-researchers.
- Submissions must adhere to a length limit of 4,400 words per article (approximately 12½ pages typed double-spaced, including illustrations and references).
- *Everything* in the manuscript must be typed double-spaced, including block quotations and bibliographies.
- References should be cited according to the author-date system as outlined in *The Chicago Manual of Style*.
- Graphics accompanying manuscripts must be camera ready.
- Title pages should include address and phone numbers.
- Manuscript pages should be numbered consecutively.
- Send two copies of the manuscript to the editor at the following address:

Thomas Newkirk
Editor, *Workshop*
Department of English
Hamilton Smith Hall
University of New Hampshire
Durham, New Hampshire 03824

- Include a cover letter indicating for which volume of *Workshop* the manuscript is to be considered, as well as the contributor's school address, home address, home phone number, and grade level(s).
- Enclose a stamped, self-addressed manila envelope so the manuscript can be returned, either for revision or for submission elsewhere.
- If the manuscript is accepted for publication, the author will be required to secure written permission from each student whose work is excerpted.

   This call for manuscripts may be photocopied for distribution to classroom teachers. The editor invites all interested teachers of grades K–8 to consider sharing discoveries about teaching and learning in the pages of *Workshop*.

ABOUT WORKSHOP
1, 2, and 3

*W*orkshop is an annual written by and for teachers of grades K–8, a place for teachers to share their new practices and their students' responses. The contributors are experienced teacher-researchers who avoid gimmicks and prescriptions in order to focus on how students learn the language arts and what teachers can do to help. Each *Workshop* addresses a current topic in the teaching of reading and writing. Each volume also features a discussion between an expert teacher and a professional leader, an article by a writer of children's books, and an interview with another children's author.

Workshop 1

The theme of *Workshop 1* is Writing and Literature. Its authors examine what is possible when teachers who understand real reading and writing bring them together so that students can engage in and enjoy both, draw naturally and purposefully on their knowledge of both, and discover what the authors and readers of a variety of genres actually do. A wealth of children's literature plays an essential role in their K–8 classrooms.

Readers will learn exciting new approaches to the teaching of writing and reading from teachers who understand both processes from the inside.

Contents: About *Workshop 1 Nancie Atwell* Seeking Diversity Reading and Writing from the Middle to the Edge *Linda Rief* Casey and Vera B. *Barbara Q. Faust* An Author's Perspective:

Letters from Readers *Ann M. Martin* P. S. My Real Name Is Kirstin *Daniel Meier* The Teacher Interview: Jack Wilde *An Interview by Thomas Newkirk* When Literature and Writing Meet *Donna Skolnick* A Garden of Poets *Cora Five* Everyday Poets: Recognizing Poetry in Prose *Marna Bunce* From Personal Narrative to Fiction *Kathleen A. Moore* Historical Fiction: The Tie That Binds Reading, Writing, and Social Studies *Patricia E. Greeley* We Built a Wall *Carol S. Avery* Fossil Hunters: Relating Reading, Writing, and Science *Rena Quiroz Moore* The Author Interview: Carol and Donald Carrick *An Interview by Mary Ellen Giacobbe* One of Us *Carol J. Brennan* Process and Empowerment *Karen Weinhold*

Workshop 2

The theme of *Workshop 2* is Beyond the Basal. Although there is a definite movement toward new approaches to teaching reading, basal series are still dominant, and teachers who venture beyond them are in the minority. This book is directed to teachers who want to implement a literature-based curriculum and have questions about organizing a classroom that is not dependent on the structure created by a basal program.

The contributors to *Workshop 2* are teachers who have found practical, rewarding, and effective ways to move beyond basals and to make literature, students' responses to literature, and their own knowledge the heart of reading instruction. Readers, regardless of their experience, will be encouraged to bring literature into their students' lives.

Contents: About *Workshop 2 Nancie Atwell* Stephen and *The Haunted House:* A Love Story *Barbara Q. Faust* An Author's Perspective: The Room in Which Van Gogh Lived *Cynthia Rylant* Nebuchadnezzar Meets Dick and Jane: A Reader's Memoir *Ginny Seabrook* The Silences Between the Leaves *Marni Schwartz* Responding to the Call *Kathy Matthews* Once upon a Time in Room Seven *Kathleen A. Moore* The Author Interview: Jack Prelutsky *An Interview by Kathy Hershey* Audience: Key to Writing About Reading *Cyrene Wells* Talk: Responding to Books the Collaborative Way *Adele Fiderer* The Teacher Interview: Carol Avery *An Interview by Jane Hansen* Children as Authorities on Their Own Reading *Bobbi Fisher* Writing and Reading Literature in a Second Language *Dorothy M. Taylor* Beyond Labels: Toward a Reading Program for All Students *Joan Levy and Rena Moore* Apprenticeship: At Four or Fourteen *Linda Rief*

Workshop 3

The theme of *Workshop 3* is The Politics of Process. The authors describe the efforts of teachers and administrators who have engaged in the politics of process in order to teach writing and reading as they believe they should. They have joined forces with like-minded colleagues, invited dialogue with administrators, created opportunities for parents to see their children's school experience with new eyes, developed appropriate methods of evaluating literacy, and made the community part of their responsibility as teachers.

This volume is a practical invitation to teachers and administrators who are seeking strategies that will help them gain acceptance for process approaches to writing and reading in their schools.

Contents: About *Workshop 3 Nancie Atwell*   An Invitation to Bake Bread *Linda Hazard Hughs*   A Letter to Parents About Invented Spelling *Mary Ellen Giacobbe*   An Author's Perspective: The Koala as a Teacher of Reading *Mem Fox*   Portfolios Across the Curriculum *Mark Milliken*   Evaluation: What's Really Going On? *Lynn Parsons*   A Guest Essay: The Middle Class and the Problem of Pleasure *Thomas Newkirk*   Setting the Stage *Mimi DeRose*   The Teacher Interview: Toby Kahn Curry and Debra Goodman *An Interview by Yetta Goodman with Commentary by Ken Goodman*   The Sun Does Not Set in Ganado: Building Bridges to Literacy on the Navajo Reservation *Sigmund A. Boloz*   A Guest Essay: Learning Literacy Lessons *Patrick Shannon*   "Change the Word Screw on Page 42" *Ed Kenney*   Publishing and the Risk of Failure *Marguerite Graham*   The Author Interview: Bill Martin, Jr. *An Interview by Ralph Fletcher*   On Becoming an Exemplary Teacher: Having Dinner with Carol *Margaret Lally Queenan.*